# The
# ONION BOOK

## A Bounty of Culture, Cultivation and Cuisine

Carolyn Dille and Susan Belsinger

 INTERWEAVE PRESS

# The
# ONION BOOK

## A Bounty of Culture, Cultivation and Cuisine

Carolyn Dille and Susan Belsinger

THE ONION BOOK
by Carolyn Dille and Susan Belsinger

Design, Susan Wasinger, Signorella Graphic Arts
Photography, Joe Coca, except as follows: pages 27, 29, 31, and 35, Susan Belsinger
Production, Elizabeth R. Mrofka

Interweave Press, Inc.
201 East Fourth Street
Loveland, Colorado 80537
USA

printed in Hong Kong by Sing Cheong

**Library of Congress Cataloging-in-Publication Data**

Dille, Carolyn..
    The onion book : a bounty of culture, cultivation, and cuisine / by Carolyn
Dille and Susan Belsinger.
            p.    cm.
    Includes index.
    ISBN 1-883010-10-1
    1. Cookery (Onions)    2. Onions.    I. Belsinger, Susan.    II. Title.
TX 803.O5D55 1996
641.6'525--dc20                                        95-40810
                                                            CIP

First printing: IWP—20M:1295:CC

# DEDICATION

*This book is for our parents, Robert Dille and Pearl Jones, and Robert and Audrey Belsinger, who encouraged us to taste and enjoy from the time we were babies, and to our grandmothers, Fanny Jones, Ella McCleary Bauer, and Alma Kontner Belsinger, who fostered our love of cooking in so many easy and delicious lessons when we were children.*

# ACKNOWLEDGEMENTS

*Every book we undertake demonstrates the generosity of our families, friends, and colleagues. The support we receive for our garden cookbooks calls forth our deepest gratitude: without the many that help us till, sow, and tend—particularly our husbands, who add these tasks to their own work—while we are teaching or traveling, these books would lack a depth that we hope benefits the reader. We would especially like to thank Dick Walvis, Tomaso Sargent, Deborah Hall, Sara Hinkleman, Linda Ligon, Joe Coca, and Judith Durant.*

# Table of Contents

**page 9**

FOREVER ONIONS

**page 17**

ONIONS IN THE KITCHEN

**page 25**

ONIONS
IN THE GARDEN

**page 37**

BREADS, APPETIZERS
AND FIRST COURSES

**page 46**

SOUPS AND PASTA

**page 56**

MAIN COURSES

**page 69**

VEGETABLES
AND SALADS

**page 79**

SAUCES,
ACCOMPANIMENTS,
AND CONDIMENTS

**page 89**

DESSERTS

**page 94**

BIBLIOGRAPHY
SOURCES

**page 95**

INDEX

*Pearl onions may be any variety of bulb onion planted thickly and harvested early. Shown here are yellow pearl onions.*

# FOREVER ONIONS

The humble onion (*Allium cepa*) is the vegetable kingdom's symbol of eternity, practically as well as esoterically. More onions are consumed than any other vegetable. Hundreds of thousands of dishes begin with them—whether they originated in Katmandu or Kinshasa, San Diego or Shanghai, Stockholm or Santiago. These dishes are usually time-honored ones, upon which rests a local cuisine's glory around the globe. Whether the cooking is grain-, meat-, vegetable-, or dairy-based, with whatever special local ingredients it contains, onions form the foundation. It's a safe bet that the number of recipes for soups, stews, sauces, casseroles, and braises that contain onions is much greater than those that do

not. Clearly, the art of cooking would be unrecognizable without the versatility that these vegetables allow us in the kitchen. Cooking without onions is a bit like playing a symphony without strings; it can be done, but the results do not resonate so harmoniously without the sweet and broad base they provide.

One reason onions fascinate us enough to write about them is that they are one of a dozen or so food plants (others include their cousin garlic as well as grapes, corn, chiles, and rice) whose origins and uses are prehistoric. These plants have collected a wealth of stories, myths, symbols, and culinary and medicinal uses that connects us to a deep and broad view of human activities and attitudes. Because

onion relatives are found in the wild worldwide, it is likely that the onion has been a common ingredient of the cuisines of the world from the time before humans wrote, perhaps even before they talked. Most botanists and plant and food historians consider the common bulb onion (*Allium cepa*) native to Central Asia because the first written references are from there, though no onion seed or tissue has been found fossilized. In its long and robust life with humans on the planet, the onion has found many champions, including poets, along with a few sermonizers who warn us of the hazards of unbridled or improper onion consumption. To the sixteenth-century English herbalist Gerard's contention, onions "causeth headache, hurteth the eyes, and maketh a man dimme sighted, sulleth the senses, engendereth windinesse and provoketh over-much sleepe, especially being eaten raw," we simply reply that we have not experienced such symptoms.

When the eighth-century Chinese poet Tu Fu wrote of onions, he wrote a world. From "Yuan Fang the Hermit on an Autumn Day, Thirty Bundles of Winter Onions":

*Potherbs in the autumn garden*
*round the house*
*Of my friend the hermit*
*behind his rough-cut*
*Timber gate. I never wrote*
*and asked him for them*
*But he's sent this basket*
*full of Winter Onions, still*
*Damp with dew. Delicately*
*grass-green bundles,*
*White jade small bulbs.*
*Chill threatens an*
*old man's innards,*
*These will warm and comfort me.*

Winter onions (*A. fistulosum*) are what we know as true scallions or bunching or Welsh onions, called *ciboules* by the French.

Some ancient cultures raised the onion to symbolic heights. The Romans considered the concentric rings of cut onions and globe shape of uncut ones emblematic of eternity. Although we are not onion worshippers, we, too, have noticed the beauty of onion rings and the mystery of the perfection of some onions' globe forms. The Egyptians painted or carved onion shapes on monuments and in tombs to depict their use as funeral offerings and in embalming. Both civilizations showed their practical nature in honoring the abundance of the onion and their caste-consciousness in considering it a food for the lower classes. By the first century A.D., most of Roman society had accepted and even relished onions, according to a list of varieties and flavors compiled by the Roman scholar Pliny the Elder (A.D.

SOME ANCIENT

CULTURES RAISED

THE ONION TO

SYMBOLIC HEIGHTS.

23–79). Though we can find no record of the Greeks' use of onions as decorative or symbolic motifs, Olympic athletes partook of them in ceremonies before the games to purify and condition their blood. Greek and Phoenician sailors carried onions on board ship; their goodly content of vitamin C must have helped to prevent scurvy.

## Healthful Allies

Wherever onions and their relatives have grown, wild or cultivated, people have used them to relieve coughs and colds as well as draw "poisons" from wounds and ulcers. Native American, European, and Asian folk medicine is replete with onion treatments. Susan's mother, raised in Baltimore, Maryland, remembers raw onion poultices' being used to relieve chest congestion—and their terrible smell. Her father-in-law from New England recalls onion poultices being placed

on the soles of the feet to reduce high fever from flu. In China, onion tea has been prescribed for cholera and dysentery, as well as for common fevers and headaches. Both garlic and onion juice have been mixed with honey for homemade cough syrups. Herbalists throughout history have recommended onions to treat gout and arthritis, soothe burns and speed their healing, and arrest or reverse baldness. Grating or maceration released their juices for direct application or medicinal spoonfuls. Though Gerard cautioned against eating onions, he recommended sniffing their juice to relieve congestion during a head cold.

While we don't see commercials for onion treatments replacing the expensive hair transplant ads on television, we could not find that anyone is presently studying the properties of onions that might affect baldness. Perhaps there's not

an economic incentive, or perhaps our cultural conditioning says that it's just too silly. Researchers are, however, focusing their efforts on more serious health problems and finding that onions and their relatives show promise in treating a wide range of disorders.

Studies have established that eating onions and garlic (*A. sativum*) reduce the low-density-lipoprotein (LDL) cholesterol that clogs the arteries. Further, onions' anti-clotting properties make them doubly helpful to the circulatory system. Onions have also reduced blood sugar levels in some people. Many studies demonstrated their antibacterial properties, and some against particular respiratory bacterial diseases. Researchers in China, India, Europe, and North America have conducted observational and double-blind studies of onions and garlic, and these suggest that they may play a role in preventing

*Red, yellow, and white pearl onions are festive and tasty, too.*

some stomach cancers and enhancing the immune system, though the different methodologies have left some questions.

More than 100 sulfur compounds found in onions have anti-inflammatory properties. Many are known to change readily when heated or when they are broken by cutting or pressure. According to the chemist Eric Block, "Onions contain the most bizarre and exotic sulfur compounds that have ever been made synthetically or found in nature." We'll return to the subject of sulfur often when we discuss onion preparation with and without tears, sweet onion varieties, soil conditions, and varieties that store well.

Apart from any preventive properties that alliums may have, there are plenty of good reasons to eat onions and their relatives daily. They contain substantial amounts of vitamin C, potassium, and fiber but only a trace of fat and very little sodium. Green onion tops and scallions have a high amount of vitamin A. Cooking hardly decreases the nutrient content of bulb onions and shallots (*A. cepa*, Aggregatum Group). It is still a matter of debate whether popping onion or garlic pills is as beneficial as making fresh alliums a daily part of the diet. Perhaps only the natural onion, garlic, shallot, or leek (*A. porrum*) have the right combination of enzymes, sulfides, precursors, etc. to benefit human health. On the other hand, some studies have shown that garlic and onion extracts in pill form effectively reduced LDL levels in significant numbers of people. The wisest and most pleasant course for most people is probably to include a variety of these vegetables in their diet, both raw and cooked.

## TEARS AND AROMAS

What brings tears to cooks' eyes is a rapidly changing series of events that begin when onion cells are broken. Devilishly complex and highly reactive sulfides in the onion juice dissolve in the fluids in our eyes forming a weak sulfuric acid solution which may burn or hurt. The discomfort has led to centuries of folk methods to avoid onion tears. Burnt matches held between the teeth bring comic but not actual relief for us. Keeping the mouth firmly closed is another trick that has failed us. Rinsing and refrigerating onions are methods that actually affect the tearing factor in onions: water washes away the factor, and cold makes it less volatile. Really sensitive people find that they must wear snorkeling, safety, or ski goggles to remain tearless when cutting onions. Though we don't think that crying in itself is altogether bad—it can cleanse the eyes and ease the heart—we've had enough experience with large-scale onion dicing to be glad that we haven't had to live as scullery maids or apprentice in European professional kitchens. In our restaurant and catering days, we used to have to peel and slice or dice onions by the thirty-pound case. These softball-sized food service onions were hot, hot, hot, and they invariably produced a red face, runny nose, and blinding tears in the individual who had to prepare them. In the normal amounts that we now work with for family meals and for our cookbooks, we're willing to put up with a few tears because we know that they will be transformed into satisfied sighs when we sit down to eat the final dish. We've found goggles useful, however, when working with several pounds of alliums.

The smell of cooking onions has an appeal that is practically universal and for most humans, irresistible. A friend's real estate agent advised her to have a skillet of onions sautéing during her open house to whet the appetite of potential buyers and say "home" to them. It would indeed be a poor home that did not have some member of the onion family in the refrigerator or cupboard. The affluent no-time-for-cooking single urban dweller has learned somewhere that chopped scallions can bring a measure of solace, civilization, and fresh flavor to the microwave dinner. The meal-maker on a restricted budget knows how much satisfaction, accomplishment, and savory sweetness a sautéed onion can bring to a dinner of rice and lentils, and at minimal cost. Though cooked onions appeal to most people, many shun raw onions because of their lingering effects in the breath and digestive system. Jonathan Swift recognized this eloquently in his "Market Women's Cries:"

*Come, follow me by the smell,*
*Here are delicate onions to sell*
*I promise to use you well.*
*They make the blood warmer;*
*You'll feed like a farmer:*
*For this is every cook's opinion,*
*No savoury dish without an onion:*
*But, lest your kissing*
*should be spoil'd,*
*Your onion must be*
*thoroughly boil'd. . .*

Cut raw onions that have stood for some time have an acrid taste and aroma, clearly discernible at hot-dog stands and company picnics. Rinsing the cut onions and keeping them chilled and covered helps a great deal to minimize unappetizing taste and aroma. Rinsing washes some sulfur away so that there is less to oxidize; and chilling slows the rate of oxidation, and covering keeps air from the onions. For the best flavor, eat onions within an hour or two of cutting.

As a cure for onion breath, we believe that entire nations should eat raw onions, thus avoiding the social anxiety that deprives people of the pleasure and health benefits of eating them. Most remedies, including the extreme of mouthwashes, have dubious efficacy, though people through the ages have reported good results from eating parsley and chewing anise or

coriander seeds, cloves, or coffee beans. We offer our kindest sympathy to those, including some of our friends and family, who "love raw onions, but they don't agree with me".

Are the concerns about onion breath and digestibility due to cultural conditioning or genetic predisposition? Carolyn's paternal grandfather, who worked for a time as a railroad construction foreman, used to tell with a combination of admiration and disdain of the immigrant Lithuanian and Polish workers who ate onion sandwiches for lunch. This bit of family lore didn't prevent her father from passing on to his children his love of onion-and-cucumber salad; perhaps it even encouraged him. Her maternal grandfather, when he farmed, raised onions as a cash crop, and her mother loved raw onions enough to teach her children to build beautiful sandwiches of Bermuda onion, ripe tomato, and mayonnaise, as well as to garnish dishes with sliced scallions and diced sweet onions. Researchers are far from finding a genetic marker for alliums, but we've concluded that it is helpful to be raised in an onion-loving family.

## Kissing Cousins

Among the several important branches of the edible alliums, we concentrate here on bulb onions, shallots, leeks, and scallions. We discussed garlic *(Allium sativum)* and its close relatives at length in *The Garlic Book* and we covered chives *(A. schoenoprasum)* and garlic chives *(A. tuberosum)* in *Herbs in the Kitchen* both published by Interweave Press.

Bulb onions *(A. cepa,* Cepa Group), no matter their size, shape, or color, are biennials, plants that normally set seed during their second year. They include pungent storage onions—yellow, white, and red; sweet onions—the

Granex types such as Maui, Texas Sweet 1015, Vidalia, and Walla Walla; pearl onions; boiling onions; and the flat, small onions (cipolline) that Italians like to pickle. Sweet onions, also called fresh onions, have a high water content and relatively low sulfur content, which makes them sweet but limits their storage life to a couple of months. Growers of these onions use rather expensive controlled-atmosphere coolers to extend their market season, but the home cook and gardener should consider these onions as seasonal and perishable. Pearl and boiling onions may be any variety of bulb onion; they are planted very thickly and harvested early while still small, pearl onions when 1/2 to 1 inch in diameter, and boiling onions 1 to 2 inches.

Shallots *(A. cepa,* Aggregatum Group), and their close relatives the potato onions are perennials, but we treat them as annuals and

have had good midspring crops from fall-planted shallots in northern California and Maryland. Under favorable conditions—well-drained soil and no deep-ground-freezing temperatures—they overwinter and begin to grow and divide the next spring. This characteristic gives them another name, multipliers. Potato onions are more rounded than shallots, and their leaves grow together in one sheath, whereas each shallot leaf has its own sheath. Red, yellow, and white cultivars of both kinds are available. The main difference that we have noticed is in flavor. Shallots, particularly the teardrop shaped types such as Frog's Leg and French Grey, are less pungent than potato onions and have a more complex flavor.

Leeks *(A. ampeloprasum,* Porrum group), famed as a symbol of Welsh courage and independence and so popular in Wales that they are sometimes called "poor man's as-

*Fall-sown baby leeks.*

Scallions, (*A. fistulosum*), are also called green onions or spring onions in North American markets. Seed purveyors refer to them as bunching onions and bulbless Japanese, Chinese, or Welsh onions. Red, yellow, and white cultivars are available, though most commercial markets offer only the white ones; we find red varieties sometimes at farmers' markets. Although they are available year round, their peak season is spring. Supermarket scallions may also be bulb onions which have been harvested when immature, before the bulbs begin to swell; however, leaves of scallions are round in cross section whereas those of bulb onions are flattened with one concave side. Either can be used when green onions are wanted.

paragus", are biennials. Like onions, they produce hard, solid seed stalks in their centers early during their second year, becoming tough and flavorless—in a word, inedible. The extra attention that leeks require to blanch them with mounded soil and tend them for the four months or more that many varieties need to mature—makes them more expensive than onions; however, their flavor—fuller, softer, and subtler than that of onions—is essential to many dishes and can enhance many others.

# ONIONS IN THE KITCHEN

The number of recipes that feature onions runs to exhaustive volumes. In the recipe section, we offer a sampling of old and current favorites that are both simple to make and flavorful. Here, we mention techniques, methods, and some dishes that we have enjoyed for many years. These represent different cuisines, and most come from that most delicious branch, traditional home cooking. For the most part, they are so simple that a description is all you need to duplicate them in the kitchen. For example, it is easy to make the Irish specialty "champ" by adding a bunch of thinly sliced green onions to mashed potatoes prepared according to your own favorite method. One of the very simplest onion dishes we know, perfect for anyone who likes raw onions, is the sandwich that Susan's husband, Tomaso, has been making for years: thinly sliced onions (preferably sweet, but storage will do—rinse them if you like), placed between two slices of whole wheat bread spread thickly or thinly with plain or chunky peanut butter. Tomaso came across this recipe in Ernest Hemingway's *Islands in the Stream,* which he read as a youth. The captain requested a peanut butter and onion sandwich, accompanied by a bottle of cold tea. Upon serving the captain his breakfast, the crewman remarked, "One of the highest points in the sandwich-maker's art. We call it the Mount Everest Special. For Commanders only." Tomaso has found it a wonderful traveling sandwich—good when hiking, biking, kayaking, or windsurfing—for it is tasty, packs easily, and isn't messy. Bread variations are always possible, as is using leftover grilled onions.

Scallions appear in more Asian recipes than bulb onions do; probably because of their long history of cultivation, their short growing period, and their perfect adaptability to the short cooking times and flavors of stir-fry cooking. For a delicious Chinese-style enhancement to clear broths, even those that are not strictly Asian, add three or four thin scallions tied in a simple loop knot to the prepared broth and simmer for several minutes before removing the knot and adding other ingredients. Knead the scallions gently with your fingers to limber them enough to tie easily. The scallion knot also adds a subtle onion flavor to long-simmered dishes of any provenance when you wish a subtle onion flavor.

Of course, scallions are not overlooked in other regions of the world. Any cooks who have devised egg dishes—omelets, frittatas, kookoos (Persian soufflés)—have found a way to incorporate scallions into them. Because scallions are usually mild, they are one of the classic raw vegetable nibbles. One of our friends recalls dipping them in a salt cellar at the beginning of many meals when he was a child. They garnish dishes from all continents, even some sweet puddings from Asia.

The cuisines of Thailand, Cambodia, Indonesia, and Singapore use fried shallots and bulb onions as garnishes. These are wonderful with cooked vegetables, omelets, baked, grilled, or broiled fish, and chicken braises and curries. Thinly sliced raw shallots also appear in Thai and Cambodian salads. To prepare the garnishes, slice shallots thinly and separate the rings. Dice onions finely. Heat an inch of cooking oil in a heavy pan over medium heat. The oil is ready when a shallot ring or a few pieces of diced onion sizzle gently but firmly. Add enough shallot or onion to cover the pan without crowding and fry 30 seconds to 2 minutes, or until pale to rich golden brown, depending on your taste and preparation. Drain on paper towels. Leeks are also delicious when fried in this way. Cut the white and pale tender green part of the leeks into fine julienne or thin rings. Because all of these alliums contain sugars and sulfur compounds, they will burn or turn from perfectly done to overcooked and acrid in less than a second. To prevent this sad outcome, watch them carefully, turn them frequently, and remove them to drain the moment that they are done as you like.

In France, shallots are the preferred allium for sauces. They are often cooked, sometimes softened but not browned, and featured raw in some vinaigrettes and the classic oyster sauce mignonette. Mignonette is also good with other bivalves on the half shell, and we like it with sweet spot prawns and crayfish that have been steamed or grilled. The most common formulation is equal parts white wine and white wine vinegar, about one-quarter by volume of finely diced shallots, and cracked black pepper to taste. The proportions can be varied according to the strength of the vinegar, wine, and shallots. Some cooks steep the shallots overnight, then strain the sauce before serving, but most simply make and chill the sauce about an hour before using it. Another French specialty is shallots poached in red wine as an accompaniment to roast or grilled beef. All of the alliums featured in this book are excellent with red wine. Add a pinch each of salt and sugar to some good but not expensive wine such as Zinfandel or Merlot and perhaps a tarragon sprig, then simmer blanched and peeled shallots (or baby onions) until they are crisp-tender. They make an unusual and tasty addition to an hors d'oeuvres tray of mixed meats, cheeses, and vegetables or vegetables alone.

Soubise (onion sauce) is an old-fashioned French preparation that takes some time, but it is delicious; we like to find a rainy or winter day when we can combine sauce-making with other indoor activities. To make soubise, slice about two pounds of onions and stew them gently in some butter about half an hour, or until they are soft. Whisk in a white sauce made with milk

*The number of recipes that feature onions runs to exhaustive volumes. Vidalias are shown here.*

or chicken or veal broth. Season with salt, pepper, nutmeg, a pinch of cayenne or dash of bitters, and barely simmer for 10 minutes. Puree the sauce in a blender or food processor. Soubise is good with plain cauliflower, brussel sprouts, Belgian endive, and boiled roast beef and makes a fine savory soufflé base. It freezes well.

In France, the leek is queen of the stockpot. Leeks are also dished up in salads of leeks à la grecque and leeks à la vinaigrette, and an important element of vichyssoise (cold leek and potato soup) which was invented by a French chef working in the United States. Cooking large whole leeks by blanching, steaming, or braising is a bit chancy. Storage leeks, even when they are not overgrown—those giants a cooking colleague calls horse leeks—do not cook evenly. The translucent skin between the layers of flesh rapidly becomes slimy in

moist-heat cooking while any green tissue, whether pale or dark, and sometimes even the white remains unpleasantly undercooked and stringy. We indulge our leek salad cravings with leeks that are between 1/2 and 3/4 inch thick. Moist heat cooks these fresh and small leeks thoroughly (we like to leave a little of the tougher dark green leaves for color in presentation). Pencil-sized leek thinnings are a seasonal treat raw in salads, either sliced thinly or julienned.

Larger leeks are best cooked by cutting them and sautéing them in a bit of butter or oil, after which they may be incorporated into any number of soups, pies or tarts, casseroles, or sautéed vegetable mixtures, or used as a base for baked or braised meat, chicken, and fish dishes. A version of Scotch broth that we particularly like contains a good portion of softened leeks along with carrots, celery, and barley that

THE CUISINES OF

THAILAND, CAMBODIA,

INDONESIA, AND

SINGAPORE USE FRIED

SHALLOTS AND BULB

ONIONS AS GARNISHES.

have been cooked in lamb stock. Cock-a-leekie is another traditional Scottish soup. Simmer a stewing hen, if you can find one, or cook a roaster in beef or chicken broth with a bouquet garni and three or four leeks. When the meat is falling from the bones, remove the chicken, leeks, and bouquet garni, then strain and defat the broth. Puree the cooked leeks and return them to the broth together with additional leeks diced and softened, the chicken meat, and diced, pitted prunes. Simmer the soup for 15 minutes longer. This dish has many variations, including one without the addition of leeks, and one with rice instead of prunes.

Leeks, shallots, onions, scallions, and green onions are all excellent when grilled. Cooking time varies according to type and size. Leave some outer layers on leeks and shallots, and discard the blackened layers just before eating. These layers retain moisture and keep the tender inner flesh from becoming bitter. Sweet onions are the most forgiving type to grill; their relatively high sugar content makes them tend to caramelize rather than burn. Scallions and green onions need a very short time on the grill; just enough to mark and scent them with smoke. When grilling any of the alliums, use a moderate fire, brush the vegetables with oil or an oil-based marinade, and turn them frequently. They are wonderful partners to other grilled vegetables and can accompany any of the usual meat, fish, and chicken grills, as well as room-temperature semisoft cheeses such as chèvre, feta, brie types, fontina, or bel paese. We also like them as pizza and pasta toppings.

## CUTTING AND CRYING

The most important tool for reducing onions, shallots, and leeks to recipe readiness is a sharp knife. The sharper the knife, the faster the slicing or dicing goes, and the less exposure the cook has to the free-floating tear-producing molecules. Chilling the onions for at least eight hours before cutting reduces the volatility of the tearing factor but is not always feasible. What works best for us is plentiful rinsing after trimming the ends and again, if necessary, after peeling and cutting the onion in half. Rinsing also rids the onion of harsh-tasting compounds. This method works as well with shallots, leeks, and green onions, too.

Look for milky juices when you trim the ends—the stronger the onion, the whiter the juices will be. Those of sweet onions are clear. Rinse milky juices away quickly with cold water and sponge down your work surface and knife. Stand back a bit from the onions rather than bending directly over them: the lacrimatory molecules have farther to go to reach your eyes. Peeling and cutting onions under water is effective in preventing tears but awkward.

The time-honored method and quickest way to dice onions is to start by cutting very thin slices from the root and stem ends. Halve the onions from stem to root, peel them, then place the flat surfaces on the cutting board. Holding the knife parallel to the board and starting at the stem end, cut nearly to the root, which holds the onion together, in horizontal slices as thick as you want your dice to be. Then cut vertical slices as thick as the horizontal ones, taking care not to cut into the root end. Finally, slice crosswise to make perfect dice. Shallots can be diced very finely by this technique using a paring knife. Cutting halved onions with the flat surface down is also the fastest way to cut slices.

To trim and clean leeks, begin by cutting off the roots and most of the dark green leaves. The leaves may be used in stocks and soup bases. Discard the outer layer or two of flesh. Hold the leek at about a 30-degree angle to the cutting board and cut about 1½ inches of the leafy end toward the board, rotating as you cut to end up with a feathered pencil-point shape. This operation trims the remaining tough outer leaves. Next, place the leek on the board and make a lengthwise cut 2 to 3 inches long in the trimmed leafy end. Rinse the leek in or under cold water, fanning the leafy ends to release any soil caught between the layers. You may have to peel another layer or two to get rid of the soil. The rinsed leeks, may be sliced in rounds, half-rounds, quarters or smaller sections, or julienned.

Though many recommend storing dry onions and shallots outside the refrigerator, it is perfectly possible to keep them there if you have the space. Typical refrigerator temperatures (35° to 40°F (1° to 4°)) and humidity (60 to 70 percent) are perfect storage conditions for onions. If unpeeled onions and shallots are kept in mesh bags outside of vegetable and fruit storage sections, they should keep well for several weeks. However, if the humidity control is set on high, or if you live in a hot, humid climate, the refrigerator probably will be too moist for good storage. Mold fungi attack damp onions. Do not let raw alliums freeze; they break down quickly when frozen and do not retain their flavor or texture.

For long-term harvest storage, refer to "Onions in The Garden" (page 25). We store purchased onions, a few pounds at a time, in a cool and dry place. Sprouting onions indicate that the storage area is too warm; moldy onions or ones showing root growth indicate that it is too damp. When buying onions, look for bright, shiny skins and an absence of dark or green molds and sprouts. Feel them all over for firmness, which indicates crispness; there should be no soft spots or dampness.

We store halved and peeled onions to slice for sandwiches tightly wrapped in a plastic bag in the vegetable bin. We don't store sliced or diced onions for several reasons. Onion odor will permeate plastic containers and the refrigerator space. The sulfur compounds of cut onions oxidize and produce unpleasant aromas and flavors. The texture of cut onions rapidly turns from crisp to flaccid. If, for some reason, you need to store cut onions for a few hours, rinse them well to remove sulfides, then store in ice water to cover, preferably in a glass or other nonreactive container with a tight-fitting lid.

*In France, the leek is queen of the stockpot.*

We do not chop onions in the food processor or blender because the flavor becomes acrid and the texture mushy. Many recipes for Middle Eastern and Jamaican marinades call for grated onion or onion juice in small amounts just to give a strong onion flavor that stands up to other strong herb and chile ingredients. Recipes for salad dressings, dips, and spreads often call for a teaspoon to a tablespoon of onion juice or grated onion to add flavor without the crunchy texture that a volume of diced onions would impart.

Leeks, green onions, and scallions should always be stored in the vegetable section of the refrigerator in loosely closed plastic bags. To store purchased leeks for up to two weeks, choose ones that still have some roots and are firm and shiny with no dull, limp, or yellow leaves. You may trim off all but about 3 inches of the dark green leaves to save space. Choose scallions and green onions according to the same criteria, though these more delicate vegetables will keep in prime condition for only three or four days from the time you buy them, somewhat longer if they are freshly harvested.

# ONIONS IN THE GARDEN

Onions require a little more attention than some garden crops such as lettuce or garlic, but most of this involves deciding which day-length varieties to plant, sowing them indoors, and transplanting them. At harvest, curing is an important process that requires some attention. As onions cost so little at the market, they will probably not be a first-choice crop for those gardening for an economic return. Because they take a fair amount of time to reach maturity, they may not appeal to urban gardeners with limited space. But even these gardeners may be tempted to splurge on space or grow onions in deep containers on the balcony when they discover how many varieties are available to gardeners that are never seen in the stores. Leeks must be hilled with soil or compost to obtain the best yield of white stalk, but this is not a trying or time-consuming chore. Shallots are the easiest to grow of all these alliums; like leeks, they offer some monetary savings as well as variety and superior flavor to purchased ones. Scallions are the perfect choice for those who want a quick and easy onion crop. They are so reliable from seed that even children grow them happily; nevertheless, even the earliest variety takes a little more than two months from seed to harvest.

Because alliums have very shallow root systems, fertile, well-drained and well-worked soil is a must. Loose, friable soil fosters the formation of large bulbs, and good drainage is a deterrent to underground fungal diseases. Unless your soil is already in peak condition, work liberal amounts of compost, humus, or aged manure into the top 6 to 12 inches (15 to 30 cm) (fresh manure increases the chances of bulb rot). The addition of organic matter will improve the structure of sandy as well as clay soil.

A neutral to slightly acid (pH 5.6 to 6.5) soil is best for bulb formation and flavor. Have your soil tested if you are in doubt as to its pH. Very acid soil can be neutralized with lime, alkaline soil with peat moss, ground bark, or sawdust. Work in these amendments several months before sowing seed or setting out plants or sets. Alliums need ample nutrients, particularly nitrogen and phosphorus. Many commercial onion growers apply 10-20-10 fertilizer to the soil before sowing seed.

For specifics on sowing seed and tending seedlings, see page 30.

When seedlings are 3 to 4 inches (8 to 10 cm) high, or about two weeks after setting them in the garden, begin fertilizing the plants every two to three weeks with a balanced 10-10-10 formula at half the recommended strength. We have had good results with both liquid and time-release fertilizers. During this time, it is most important to keep the onion patch weeded. The shoots are so slender and fragile that it seems unlikely that they will ever become onions, leeks, etc., even with your help; without it, they must struggle to obtain nutrients against the competition. Even after the onions seem to be growing vigorously, keep them well weeded and watered. On the plus side, we have never had a seedling bed of this family ravaged by our

usual pests—snails, slugs, earwigs, flea beetles. In fact, we have noticed a deterrent effect, particularly on rabbits and snails, when we plant the borders of garden plots with alliums, which is also a space-saving way to grow them.

Onions and leeks make their best foliage and feeder root growth during cool, wet seasons, when they have plenty of water to keep them cool and soaking up nutrients. This early growth, whether it takes place in fall or spring, is directly related to how large and well formed the onions will be at harvest. The size of the layers is determined by how well the plant is feeding.

Onions and scallions have few diseases or insect pests; leeks and shallots virtually none. (Thrips, minute sucking insects, feed on the leaves of onions and scallions, leaving white blotches, particularly during hot, dry weather. If you are growing

scallions through the summer, keep them well-watered.) Still, because disease organisms and pests can overwinter in the soil, we follow the practice of crop rotation, planting other crops for two or three years in a given spot before we plant alliums there again.

## WHAT A DIFFERENCE A DAY MAKES

The most critical factor for producing fine bulb onions is the variety's day-length requirement and how that relates to where you garden. Bulb onions are classified as long-day types, short-day types, and intermediate-day types. Long-day varieties require fourteen hours or more of daylight to initiate bulb formation. This condition is met in northerly latitudes beginning about 40°, the regions where long-day onions are grown commercially. Intermediate-day onions, which require twelve to fourteen hours of daylight

*These alliums awaiting transplant were trimmed when they became too leggy.*

during the late-spring/early-summer growing season, are grown between 40° and 32° north latitude. Short-day types begin bulbing with only eleven to twelve hours of daylight and will grow successfully only in 32° north latitudes and below. Long-day cultivars will not form bulbs in the south; the days are too short during cool weather (when onions grow best), and when they are long enough, the temperature is too high. Short-day cultivars planted in northern latitudes will begin bulb formation too early, and mature onions will be small because they did not have enough time to produce foliage and root systems, which govern the ultimate size of bulbs. Intermediate-day cultivars seem to be closer in their requirements to long-day types than to short-day types. We've learned that although we can bring some short- and long-day varieties to maturity in our gardens in Maryland and Northern California (roughly 39° and 37° north latitude, respectively), they are never large and are more prone to bolt than are intermediate-day varieties. Most long- and intermediate-day cultivars are storage onions; an exception is the sweet Walla Walla. Typically short-day cultivars are sweet. Long-day onions are sown in the ground as early as weather will permit in spring or, more commonly, started indoors in flats in winter to set out in early spring. Intermediate-day types may be sown as long-day types or in the fall to overwinter for a late spring or early summer harvest. In their recommended latitudes, short-day cultivars are always sown outdoors in fall to over-winter for early spring to early summer harvest.

Aside from day length, onions' sensitivity to changes in temperature can cause them to languish or bolt, in part because they take so long to mature, four to nine months that can span some climatic extremes. Planting too early or too late or in too cold a winter can trigger bolting or die back of over-wintering plants. In the case of die back, the tops are killed and this stunts bulb formation. Moreover, onions haven't quite been tamed;

some rogues will send up seed stalks in their first year, as growers and professors ruefully acknowledge.

The art of onion growing is judging when to sow or transplant to get fine bulb size and timely bulb formation, but even professional onion specialists admit to factors outside the grower's control. As the National Garden Bureau puts it, "Some onions are less susceptible to bolting than others but the cause of bolting is complicated and not fully understood. . . The onion is a cagey character, very difficult to predict." Still, the experts offers the following tips for cultivating overwintered onions. The plants should have three leaves and be about the size diameter of a pencil when light frosts begin in your area. If they have grown to five leaves or more, they may bolt during the spring. It usually takes some trial-and-error sowings for two or three seasons to establish the best time to sow for overwintering. If frequent or deep frosts occur in your intermediate-day area, choose cultivars that are tolerant to frosts.

## KNOWING YOUR ONIONS

As the folk saying has it, someone who knows her onions is an expert in a particular field, or about life in general. That expert-making teacher, experience, will show you what you need to know about onions in your garden; however, as we and other gardeners have noticed through the years, onions—as well as leeks and shallots—can surprise you. For us, some surprises have come from purchased sets or plants that all bolted. Sets are long-day onions that have been grown to about 1/2 to 3/4 inch in (1 to 2 cm) diameter by sowing the seeds close together, selective thinning, and withholding fertilizer, (the same procedures used to produce pearl onions). They are

*Early spring onions.*

stored and sold the next season to shorten the time to harvest. In choosing sets, be aware that those larger than 3/4 of an inch (2 cm) may bolt and those smaller than 1/2 (1 cm) inch may produce small bulbs. Onion plants are also grown the previous season, but they are harvested before the bulbs swell; they look like mini-mini scallions. They are sometimes sold in garden centers in six-

packs and are available from seed suppliers in bundles that are shipped bare root for proper planting times according to region.

We have had the most reliable results—and the most choices for color, flavor, shape, and size—by growing onions, leeks, and scallions from seed. We have sometimes also bought onion sets or plants in early fall to plant for a midwinter, early spring harvest of scallions, although gardeners in northern climates could not do this. Shallot sets of different varieties for both fall and spring plantings are becoming increasingly available. We have tried many of these and found them to be satisfactory.

Growing from seed is always our first choice for several reasons. Perhaps the most important is the plain fun and sense of renewal that the seed-to-plant cycle gives us: tiny, inert-looking bits of matter become, with care, 2-foot-tall leeks or even larger cabbages or chile pepper plants. Others include the diversity of flavor and adaptability to region, the option of open-pollinated versus hybrid varieties, and the availability of heirloom and organically grown seed. Few varieties of onions, scallions, and leeks are available as plants or sets.

Though seed is dramatically less expensive than sets or plants, most garden-ers who grow long-day onions also invest in seed flats, sterile potting medium, a greenhouse, fluorescent lights, and perhaps a bottom-heating system; these all help to produce good crops in regions in which growing seasons otherwise keep the plants from maturing. With these aids, onion and leek seeds can be sown indoors in late January or February to have well-grown seedlings ready for transplanting to the garden as soon as the weather permits. Scallions may also be sown indoors in this way for early crops; seed directly in the ground when spring weather is settled for successive crops.

Sow onion, leek, or scallion seed sparingly 1/4 to 1/2 inch (5 mm to 1 cm) deep in a moist, sterile, soilless potting medium in flats that are at least 2 inches (5 cm) deep. Keep the medium between 60° and 70°F (16 and 21°C) until the seeds germinate. Place lights 6 to 8 inches (15 to 20 cm) above the flats and leave them on for at least twelve hours a day. An automatic timer can take care of turning the lights on and off. Raise the lights as the seedlings grow and fertilize lightly every two weeks with a 10-10-10 liquid fertilizer used at half strength until transplanting time, when the seedlings are 4 to 6 inches (10 to 15 cm) tall. Keep the medium as damp as a well-wrung sponge. During the week before you set them in the garden, gradually accustom them to being outdoors, starting with a few hours and increasing it until they stay outside overnight.

Shallots, onions, and scallions may be grown in rows or in space-saving beds or plots. Leeks are best grown in rows to facilitate blanching the stalks as they grow. We sow leeks rather thickly outdoors and eat the thinnings. We transplant the seedlings to small trenches 3 to 4 inches (8 to 10 cm) deep when they are 4 to 6 inches (10 to 15 cm) tall, setting them about 4 inches apart. As they grow, we gradually fill in the trench and hill soil against the stalks.

Many gardeners are thrilled when they find sweet onion varieties that will grow well in their area, then are disappointed when the onions that they harvest are hot. The main cause of hotness in sweet onions is the presence of sulfur in the soil or water. To avoid soil sulfur, grow the onions in raised beds with purchased topsoil, compost, or a mix of half compost and half topsoil. Be sure that the topsoil you buy has a low sulfur content, as well being loamy and free of weed seeds. Ask your supplier for a soil analysis. If your water supply is high in sulfur, there is little you can do short of installing a large tank for holding rainwater that you will use to water your onions. Vidalia, Georgia, and surrounding coun-

*Tall "Tree" onions are also known as "Egyptian" and "Walking Stick".*

ties are well situated for growing sweet onions, having sandy loam that is very low in sulfur.

In addition to the many varieties of alliums that we have discussed in some detail, two others are of interest to the gardener and cook. *Allium cepa,* Proliferum Group, has a number of colorful common names: Egyptian onion, topset, walking, and tree onion. The rationale for "Egyptian" seems to be lost, but the remaining appellations refer to the plant's growth and reproductive habits, as does "proliferum", its Latin name. The perennial plant sets bulbils on top rather than seed. Its many shoots look rather like coarse scallion tops and should be harvested when young, as they are tougher and have a stronger flavor than scallions. The bulbils are quite pungent and can be used like garlic. If you have space for this plant, its unusual appearance is perhaps the best reason to have it. As one of our professional herb-growing friends says, "Once you have tree onions, you will have them forever." The heads of bulbils atop their stalks put on the show of sending scallionlike shoots 2 to 3 feet (60 to 90 cm) from the ground; then the stalks eventually bend to the ground in hoops (which accounts for the "walking" designation), and the bulbils take root there. Egyptian onion is cold-hardy to about -20° F (-29°C).

Ramps (*A. tricoccum*), resemble leeks, giving rise to their common name of wild mountain leeks. Their flavor is very pungent—some say stinky—something like garlic and leeks together with a touch of wild bitterness. Ramps are not cultivated; they appear in the wild in rich woods and mountains of eastern North America. Their interest for the cook is in the several festivals that attend their appearance in the Appalachians in April and May. If you are in Helvetia, West Virginia, on the last Saturday of April, you can attend the community's Ramp Supper, which features ramps as a vegetable accompaniment to cornbread and ham. A similar supper, the Feast of the Ramson, takes place in Richwood, West Virginia, in mid-April. Cosby, Tennessee, celebrates its Ramp Festival the first Sunday in May. There whole ramps, bulbous stems and leaves, are cooked with scrambled eggs and served with fatback and fried cornbread. (One restaurateur we've heard of will not use his kitchen and dining room for ramp festivities because it takes six months for the smell to disappear from the curtains.)

Following is a list of some of our favorite allium varieties. We like these for their flavor, reliability for seed, vigor even in adverse growing conditions, yield, and, in some cases, handsome appearance. In choosing varieties for your garden, be sure to check day-length requirements for bulb onions and recommended planting times for shallots, leeks, and scallions. Of the bulb and pickling onions, Torpedo Bottle, Stockton Red, Walla Walla, Stuttgarter, Blanco Duro, Crystal Wax, Early Aviv Pearl, and Borettana Cipolline have done well in our gardens. We have excellent shallot crops from sets of French Red, French Grey, Dutch Yellow, Red Sun, Golden Gemet, and Frog's Leg. Shallots' close relatives, potato onions, are also reliable from sets. Among the leeks, we particularly like Fall Giant, Titan, Giant Winter, King Richard, which produced long stalks even without being hilled, and Bleu de Solaise for its beautiful purple-tinged foliage. In the scallion group, Emerald Isle, Tokyo Long White, White Lisbon, and Red Beard are tasty and reliable, though Red Beard produces a bluish pink outer layer rather than being red throughout.

## Harvesting, Curing, Storing

Any seedlings, plants, or sets of bulb onions may be planted to harvest as green onions or scallions, before their bulbs begin to swell; some commercial scallions are produced this way. If you plant sets, sort out those more than 3/4 inch (2 cm) or less than 1/2 (1 cm) inch across and plant them in a separate section to harvest as scallions. Keep an eye on your bulb onion and leek plants; harvest any that send up seed stalks and eat them right away unless you are planning to save the seed (in which case, let the seed heads mature). Seed stalks quickly become hard, woody, and inedible, but if you harvest the onions or leeks when the first stalks form, you can still have a fair amount of edible flesh. Thinnings of pencil-size leeks are tasty uncooked in green or vegetable salads, and thumb-size leeks are excellent when cooked. Shallots harvested while their tops are still green are a gourmet treat; to best appreciate their delicate flavor, use them raw in salads or as garnishes. Pick scallions at any size, but be aware that you will lose at least one layer of flesh to trimming.

The variety of bulb onions, and the care with which you harvest and cure onions and shallots will determine how well they will store. Sweet onions such as Granex, Maui, Texas/Sweet 1015, and Walla Walla keep for about two months in home storage conditions. Hybridization done during the past decade has developed onions that are fairly sweet yet will keep for several months. Sweet Sandwich is one such success, a long-day hybrid that actually sweetens in storage. For long-term storage, choose varieties such as Blanco Duro, Stuttgarter, Ebenezer, Red Creole, Yellow Torque, and Yula—and be prepared for pungency.

As onion bulbs reach maturity, the green tops will begin to wither and fall over. When about half of the tops in your patch have fallen naturally, you may push over the remaining tops to speed their maturation. Doing this gently, with your hands or the back of a rake, will minimize damage to the necks of the bulbs, though some commercial growers walk on the onions. Our publisher notes that everyone walked the onion fields to knock down the leaves when she was growing up in Oklahoma. Plan to harvest the bulbs within two weeks of pushing down the tops and begin withholding water to begin curing the bulbs while they are in the ground.

Curing onions and shallots is a most important part of the harvest. Onions must be allowed to dehydrate slowly so that their outer skins and necks dry completely. If they are not cured, bacteria and fungi can enter damp areas, particularly through the necks, and cause rot in the bulbs. The plants need at least five days of sunshine in a row; if it rains, cover the onions and start over. Don't wait to harvest until the tops rot; they should be limp but may be either dry or still green. If your soil is friable, you can pull the onions out by their tops. If it's not and you need a garden fork to loosen the soil, keep the tines well away from the bulbs to avoid bruising or piercing them. One or two days of curing on the ground can be done in hot, sunny weather. In very hot climates, fold the tops over the bulbs to prevent sunscald. Protect the onions from rain or dew. If the weather is very rainy, forget about trying to cure onions outdoors and move them to screens in a garage or other

CURING ONIONS AND

SHALLOTS IS A MOST

IMPORTANT PART OF

THE HARVEST.

*Assorted alliums being dried on a screen.*

dry place. Finish curing the pulled onions by spreading them in one layer on screens or baskets that allow good air circulation. Move them to a dry shady place for about two weeks to complete the curing. Sort cured onions according to the thickness of their necks; those with thick necks are more likely to mold and should therefore be used first.

Shallot tops fall over more uniformly than those of onions; we have not had to push any over. Keep the shallots dry for five days to a week after the tops have fallen. Pull them or carefully dig them and cure them like onions. Because they are smaller, shallots need less curing time than onions, about two or three days outside and a week inside, but the result is the same: well-shriveled necks and dry skins that inhibit the entrance of molds.

You may store cured onions in braids or clip the tops to 1 or 2 inch (2 or 5 cm) stubs and place the onions one or two layers deep in boxes or in mesh bags holding up to ten pounds. Alternatively, you can drop onions into the legs of old panty hose and tie knots to separate individual onions: cut below the knots to retrieve the onions.

The ideal storage conditions for onions are a temperature of 35°F (2°C) and

60 percent humidity, similar to those of a home refrigerator. If you have an extra refrigerator in which to store onions, place them in mesh, not plastic bags, or loose in the vegetable bins. Otherwise, a cool, dry place such as a garage or well-insulated basement will do. If new roots appear on stored alliums, the humidity is too high; if the tops sprout, the temperature is too high. We clip the tops of our shallots and store them in flat baskets or pint plastic berry containers.

Harvesting leeks and scallions is a matter of pulling them at the size at which you like to eat them. Many leek varieties are very cold-hardy, and so gardeners in northern latitudes can leave them in the ground to harvest through the winter as necessary. We have read about a gardener who harvests all his leeks, cuts off the roots and trims the tops down to about 3 inches (8 cm) of green leaf before storing the leeks loose in refrigerator vegetable bins for as long as three months. Scallions are quite frost-tender. Because they break off rather easily in any soil but the most friable, use a trowel to pry them out. Since they are easy to grow, we like to direct-sow them at two-week intervals for succession crops. Northern gardeners can usually count on the last crop from a first-week-in-August sowing. Mild-winter growers can make a mid-September to mid-October sowing for late winter or very early spring harvests.

There is a chicken-and-egg relationship between gardening and cooking: does harvesting lead to delicious inspirations in the kitchen (what shall we do with all those lovely leeks?), or does knowing that a baby leek salad is so tasty lead us to digging, tilling, and planting? A definitive answer may not exist, as is so often the case in the most rewarding mystery questions; we invite you to partake of the fruits of some of our explorations, guided by considerations of flavor and fun, in the recipes that follow.

# BREADS, APPETIZERS, AND FIRST COURSES

*Green Onion Focaccia*

# Green Onion Focaccia

Makes 1 10-by-12-inch (25-by-30-cm) focaccia
Serves 4 to 6

*This focaccia is inspired by the work of the Liguria Bakery in San Francisco's Washington Square. Since 1911, members of the Soracco family have been making supremely simple and satisfying focaccie: plain, brushed with olive oil; tomato, brushed with tomato sauce; and onion, brushed with tomato sauce and sprinkled with green onions. We think that the family would approve this recipe, devised for those times when we can't get to the Liguria. The dough is our tried-and-true pizza dough; the recipe will make two thin-crust pizzas about 10 inches in diameter or four individual thin-crust pizzas. Traditional Italian focaccie are*

## Pizza / Focaccia Dough

2 teaspoons (10 ml) active dry yeast
1½ cups (360 ml) water
3½ cups (830 ml) unbleached white flour

1/2 cup (120 ml) whole wheat flour, or use another 1/2 cup (120 ml) white flour if desired
2 tablespoons (30 ml) olive oil
1 teaspoon (5 ml) salt

Dissolve the yeast in 1/4 cup (60 ml) warm water. When the yeast has softened and become foamy, in about 10 minutes, add it to the rest of the water.

Mix the flours in a bowl and make a well in the mixture. Gradually stir the water and yeast into the well. Add the olive oil and salt. Gather the dough and knead it for 7 or 8 minutes, or until it is soft and lively.

Let the dough double in bulk in a lightly oiled, covered bowl; either at room temperature or, ideally, in the refrigerator overnight. Punch the dough down and pat it into a rough rectangle. Let it rest in a warm place, covered with a towel, on a lightly floured surface for 20 minutes, or until it has relaxed enough to stretch easily.

Meanwhile, preheat the oven with a baking stone for 30 minutes at 450°F (230°C), or for 15 minutes at 400°F (200°C) if you are baking on metal pans.

## Topping and Assembly

Semolina or cornmeal for sprinkling

3 tablespoons (45 ml) tomato paste

1 tablespoon (15 ml) water

About 1 tablespoon (15 ml) olive oil

4 green onions, trimmed to 3 inches (8 cm) of green and thinly sliced

*between 1½ to 2 inches (4 to 5 cm) thick and made with white flour.*

If you are using a stone, sprinkle a pizza paddle lightly with semolina or cornmeal. Otherwise, choose a metal baking sheet that measures at least 10 by 15 inches (25 by 38 cm). Sprinkle it lightly with semolina or cornmeal. With your hands, stretch the dough gently on the pizza paddle or baking sheet to a rectangle 10 by 12 inches (25 by 30 cm), and about 3/4 inch (2 cm) thick. Make dimples in the dough with your fingers or knuckles.

Slide the dough onto the baking stone, or place the baking sheet in the oven and bake for 10 minutes.

Meanwhile, place the tomato paste in a small dish and stir in 1 tablespoon water (15 ml) and 1 tablespoon (15 ml) olive oil. Mix well.

Remove the dough from the oven and brush it with the tomato paste mixture. Scatter the green onions over the top. Return the focaccia to the oven and bake for 10 to 15 minutes longer, or until the bottom is slightly crusty. Remove to a rack to cool before cutting and serving. Brush the edges with additional olive oil if desired. Serve warm or at room temperature.

# FOCACCIA WITH ONIONS AND ROSEMARY

Makes two 10-by-12-inch (25-by-30-cm) focaccie
Serves 8 to 12

*When you're in the mood for a hearty focaccia, caramelized onions with a hint of rosemary may be the perfect topping. The olives add a nice, salty, tangy contrast to the sweetness of the onions. Sometimes we omit the olives and sprinkle a little balsamic vinegar over the finished focaccia instead. Another satisfying variation is to crumble a small amount of gorgonzola on top. The topping is easily halved if you want to make only one focaccia.*

2 recipes pizza/focaccia dough, page 38

7 tablespoons (150 ml) extra-virgin olive oil

4 medium onions, quartered lengthwise and thinly sliced

2 tablespoons (30 ml) minced fresh rosemary

Salt and freshly ground pepper

2 garlic cloves, minced

About 1/2 cup (120 ml) pitted Kalamata olives, optional

Preheat the oven with a baking stone on the middle rack for 30 minutes at 500°F (260°C) or for 15 minutes at 400°F (200°C) if you are baking on metal pans. If you are using a stone, sprinkle a pizza paddle lightly with semolina or cornmeal. Otherwise, choose metal baking sheets that measure at least 10 by 15 inches (25 by 38 cm). Sprinkle them lightly with semolina or cornmeal. With your hands, stretch each portion of dough gently on the paddle or baking sheet to a rectangle 10 by 12 inches (25 by 30 cm), and 3/4 inch (2 cm) thick. Make dimples in the dough with your fingers or knuckles.

Heat 5 tablespoons (75 ml) of the olive oil over medium heat in a large sauté pan. Add the onions and stir over medium heat 5 minutes. Add the rosemary and salt and pepper to taste and stir occasionally 5 minutes longer, or until the onions turn golden. Remove the pan from the heat.

Slide the dough onto the baking stone or place the baking sheets in the oven and bake for 10 minutes.

Place the minced garlic in a shallow dish and drizzle it with the remaining olive oil.

Brush each portion of dough with the olive oil and garlic, letting some collect in the depressions. Spread the onion and rosemary mixture evenly over the focaccie.

If you are baking on a stone, slide one focaccia onto the middle of the stone. Bake it for 20 to 25 minutes, or until the bottom is slightly crusty. Remove it to a rack to cool before cutting and serving. Bake the remaining focaccia in the same way. If you are baking both focaccie on baking sheets at the same time, switch their positions about halfway through baking.

Garnish the focaccie with olives and brush the edges with additional olive oil if desired. Serve warm or at room temperature.

# BUTTERMILK BISCUITS WITH
# SCALLIONS AND PARMESAN CHEESE

About 2 dozen biscuits

*Buttery-rich tasting and full of scallion flavor, these biscuits need no extra butter. Serve them just as they are with soups and stews, and for a nice sweet-savory twist, with preserves at breakfast or brunch.*

2 cups (475 ml) unbleached flour
1/2 teaspoon (2 ml) salt
1½ teaspoons (7 ml) baking powder
1/2 teaspoon (2 ml) baking soda
Dash cayenne pepper
1/4 teaspoon (1 ml) Hungarian paprika
1/2 cup (120 ml) freshly grated parmesan cheese

5 tablespoons (75 ml) unsalted butter
1 cup (250 ml) nonfat or low-fat buttermilk
1 bunch scallions, trimmed to about 3 inches (8 cm) of green and thinly sliced

Preheat the oven to 400°F (200°C). Combine the flour, salt, baking powder, baking soda, cayenne, paprika, and cheese in a large bowl and blend thoroughly. Cut in the butter until the mixture resembles a coarse meal.

In a small bowl, combine the buttermilk with the scallions. Add the liquid to the dry ingredients and stir to form a soft dough.

Turn the dough onto a floured pastry marble or board, knead gently until it just comes together, and roll out 1/2-inch (1 cm) thick. Cut the dough into 2-inch (2.5-cm) squares, diamonds, or rounds and place them on an ungreased baking sheet.

Bake the biscuits 15 to 18 minutes, or until light golden brown. Remove to a baking rack to cool slightly. The biscuits are best served still warm from the oven, but you may prepare them in advance, cool them completely, and store them in an airtight container; wrap them in foil and gently reheat at 325°F (160°C) for 10 to 15 minutes.

# MAUI ONION TART

2 cups (475 ml) unbleached flour

8 tablespoons (120 ml) unsalted butter

2 tablespoons (30 ml) vegetable shortening

1/2 teaspoon (2 ml) salt

Large pinch sugar

1 to 2 tablespoons (15 to 30 ml) ice water

2 pounds (900 g) Maui or other sweet onions

Salt and freshly ground pepper

*This tart is a pure and simple celebration of the caramel-sweet flavor of low-sulfur onions such as Mauis. We have served it as an appetizer, as a main course for lunch with a salad, and as a dessert with thin shavings of aged gouda or sharp cheddar cheese accompanied, naturally, by a glass of wine.*

In a food processor, combine flour, 6 tablespoons (90 ml) butter, vegetable shortening, salt, and sugar, and process until coarse and crumbly. With the motor running, add water until the dough starts to come together, but doesn't form a ball. Turn the dough onto a flat surface and gather it together in a ball. Flatten it, wrap it in plastic, and refrigerate for at least 30 minutes.

Peel the onions, halve them lengthwise, and slice them thinly crosswise. Melt 2 tablespoons (30 ml) butter over medium heat in a large sauté pan. Sauté the onions over medium-low heat, stirring occasionally for 30 minutes, or until the sugars in the onions have caramelized to golden brown. Season well with salt and pepper.

Preheat the oven to 375°F (190°C). Roll the dough out on a lightly floured surface to a rectangle 12 by 14 inches (30 by 36 cm). Place the rectangle on a baking sheet and spread the onions over it, leaving 1 1/2-inches (4 cm) uncovered on each of the long sides. Fold the long sides over an inch or two (2 to 5 cm).

Bake the tart for 30-35 minutes, or until it is golden brown. Cut it diagonally into long, triangular wedges and serve.

# Chèvre with Shallots

*Our families and guests love the range of flavors in this appetizer. Choose log shapes that are 5 to 6 inches (13 to 15 cm) long. If only shorter ones are available, hollow more cheese from the center of the halved logs. Fill the cavities as indicated below, but don't place the halves together. You may hollow the logs, fill them, roll them tightly in plastic wrap, and store them in the refrigerator as long as 24 hours. Roll them in shallots and herbs as long as 4 hours before serving, cover them loosely, and return them to the refrigerator until serving time.*

2 chèvre logs, 5 to 5 1/2 ounces (140 to 155 g) each
2 large shallots, minced
2 tablespoons (30 ml) minced, oil-packed sun-dried tomatoes
Freshly ground pepper
2 tablespoons (30 ml) minced pitted

Kalamata olives
2 tablespoons (30 ml) chopped parsley
2 teaspoons (10 ml) chopped fresh marjoram or oregano
1 baguette, sliced 1/4 inch (5 mm) thick, and lightly toasted

Halve the logs lengthwise and hollow 1/2 inch (1 cm) from the center of each section with the tip of a small spoon. Reserve the extra cheese. Mix one-fourth of the shallots with the sun-dried tomatoes and season with pepper. Fill two cheese halves with the mixture; press them together to surround the tomatoes; roll them back into a log. Spread about half of the extra cheese over the seams where the sections meet. Repeat the procedure with the remaining cheese halves, one-third of the remaining shallots, and the olives.

Mix the remaining shallots with the parsley and the marjoram or oregano. Roll each log in the mixture to coat it completely. Cover them loosely and refrigerate for an hour, or until ready to serve. Slice the logs 1/4 inch (5 mm) thick and serve with the baguette toasts.

# ONION RINGS, CHESAPEAKE STYLE

Serves 3 or 4 as an appetizer or side dish

1 large sweet onion, 12 to 14 ounces
(340 to 400 g)
About 2 cups (475 ml) milk, mixed
with 2 pinches of salt
1½ cups (360 ml) unbleached flour

2 tablespoons (30 ml) Chesapeake
Bay seafood seasoning plus more
for garnish
About 2 cups (475 ml) vegetable oil

*The Chesapeake Bay region is known for its spicy seafood seasonings and light fried foods; the seafood seasoning is an excellent flavoring for onion rings. No batter here—just a dusting of well-seasoned flour and a quick fry in hot oil. Real onion-ring lovers might like to double this recipe.*

Peel the onion and slice it crosswise 3/8 to 1/2 inch (6 to 8 mm) thick. Separate the rings and place them in a large shallow dish. Pour the milk and salt over the onions, adding more milk if necessary to just cover them. Let stand for at least an hour and as long as 3 hours.

Place the flour and seasoning in a bag and shake well to mix. Heat the oil in a deep fryer over medium-high heat until it is hot but not smoking, 365°F (185°C); it should be at least 1½ inches (4 cm) deep.

A few at a time, take onion rings out of the milk, drop them in the bag of seasoned flour, and shake. Remove the coated onions from the flour and gently drop them in the oil, turning them once as they turn golden.

When the onions are light golden brown, remove them from the oil, drain them on paper towels, and sprinkle them with Chesapeake Bay seafood seasoning while they are still hot. Keep the fried onion rings warm in the oven while you fry another batch or eat them right away. They are best when served while still hot.

# SOUPS AND PASTA

*Sauté of Leeks, Endive, and Radicchio with Linguine*

# LEEK AND CHICK-PEA SOUP

Serves 4 to 6

1/2 pound (225 g) chick-peas
1 bunch tender leeks, about 1 1/2
　　pounds (700 g)
1 medium yellow or white onion
3 large garlic cloves

About 1/3 cup (80 ml) extra-
　　virgin olive oil
5 sprigs Italian parsley
2 or 3 sprigs marjoram
Salt and freshly ground black pepper

Soak the chick-peas in cold water overnight in a nonreactive soup pot. Drain, rinse, and cover with fresh water. Bring to a boil, reduce the heat, and simmer about an hour, or until very tender. Puree half the chick-peas (or more for a smoother-textured soup). Return them to the pot and salt well.

Meanwhile, clean and trim the leeks, leaving some tender green, and slice them 1/8 inch (3 mm) thick. Dice the onion and mince the garlic. Gently cook the vegetables, covered, with 3 tablespoons (45 ml) olive oil over low heat until they have softened.

Add the vegetables to the chick-peas with 3 cups (710 ml) water. Salt and pepper lightly and simmer the soup for 30 minutes. Chop the parsley and marjoram leaves and add them to the soup. Simmer 5 minutes longer and adjust the seasoning. Add up to another cup of water if thinner soup is desired.

Serve the soup very hot, drizzled with the remaining olive oil.

*This soup is our version of an old recipe from Tuscany, where leeks and chick-peas are favorite ingredients. This recipe points up the Tuscan cook's ability to extract clear, full flavors from pure and simple ingredients, their conviction that vegetables are delicious and right without stock or broth, and their concern for digestibility. The soup is light yet flavorful and makes an excellent first course. For a heartier version, toast slices of country bread, sprinkle grated parmesan cheese on them, and place a slice in each bowl before pouring the soup over them.*

# ROASTED ONION AND CORN CHOWDER WITH POBLANO CHILE CREAM

*We like to puree only half of this hearty soup to leave some nice vegetable bites, but you may puree all of it for a smooth texture and a different presentation. In place of poblanos, substitute New Mexico or Anaheim green chiles with some heat. The soup is very good; double the recipe to ensure that you'll have leftovers.*

About 1 1/2 tablespoons (22 ml) extra-virgin olive oil

1 1/4 pounds (560 g) yellow or white onions

About 3 cups (710 ml) fresh yellow or white sweet corn kernels: 4 large ears

Salt and freshly ground pepper

8 to 10 ounces (240 to 280 g) potatoes, peeled and cut into bite-sized pieces

6 cups (1420 ml) vegetable or chicken stock

1 small red bell pepper, roasted, peeled, seeded, and chopped

1 teaspoon (5 ml) cumin seed, toasted and ground

1/2 teaspoon (2 ml) coriander seed, toasted and ground

6 to 8 poblano chiles, roasted, peeled, and seeded

1/2 cup (120 ml) sour cream or sour half-and-half (a lower fat version of sour cream)

Preheat the oven to 475°F (250°C). Oil a 9-by-13-inch (23-by-33 cm) casserole with 1/2 tablespoon (8 ml) olive oil. Peel and quarter the onions lengthwise, then slice them crosswise 1/4 inch (5 mm) thick. Place the onions in the casserole and drizzle them with the remaining olive oil. Roast them for 20 minutes, turning them once or twice. Stir in the corn and roast 10 minutes longer, stirring occasionally. Remove the onions and corn from the oven and season them with salt and pepper.

While the onions are roasting, place the potatoes and 5 cups (1220 ml) stock in a nonreactive soup pot. Cook, covered, over medium heat about 15 minutes, or until the potatoes are tender. Remove the pot from the heat. In batches in a blender, puree half the potatoes with a little stock and the roasted bell pepper. Return the puree to the soup pot.

Also in batches, puree a generous half of the onions and corn with a little stock from the soup pot. Add this puree to the soup pot with the remaining onions and corn. Rinse the blender jar with the remaining cup of stock and add it to the pot. Generously season the soup with salt and pepper and add the cumin and coriander. Stir well and cook over medium heat for 5 to 10 minutes. Adjust the seasoning.

In a blender, puree the chiles with the sour cream and a pinch of salt. Serve the hot soup in bowls garnished with the poblano cream. Pass the extra poblano cream for those who like it hot.

# Onion Family Soup

*Here is sweet allium essence in a soup that is simple to make and comforting to eat. It can precede almost any main course and is especially good before roast poultry. Its simplicity and humble ingredients notwithstanding, it is fine enough to start a company dinner. For variety, use all onions, and/or add a clove or two of minced garlic. Add a little more turmeric if its warmth appeals to you. In place of potato starch, you may use one small potato, boiled until soft, mashed, and mixed with the milk. The soup reheats well.*

1 ½ *pounds yellow or white (675 g) onions, diced*

2 *pounds (900 g) leeks, white and pale tender green part, halved crosswise and thinly sliced*

3 *shallots, diced*

3 *tablespoons (45 ml) unsalted butter*

4 *cups (950 ml) chicken or vegetable stock*

2 *cups (475 ml) milk*

2 *tablespoons (30 ml) potato starch*

1/2 *teaspoon (2 ml) ground turmeric*

*Salt and freshly ground pepper*

2 *tablespoons (30 ml) chopped chives or parsley*

Soften the onions, leeks, and shallots in the butter over low heat in a 6-quart nonreactive (6-l) soup pot. When the vegetables are soft, add the stock and simmer, covered, for 15 minutes. Puree half or all of the vegetables with a little stock and return to the pot.

Mix 1 cup (240 ml) milk with the potato starch. Gradually stir it into the soup. Mix the turmeric with the remaining cup of milk and stir it into the soup. Season with salt and pepper. Simmer the soup for 10 minutes. Serve the soup hot, garnished with chopped chives or parsley.

# ITALIAN-STYLE BREAD AND ONION SOUP

5 tablespoons (75 ml) unsalted butter

3 tablespoons (45 ml) extra-virgin olive oil

3 pounds (1.4 kg) yellow onions, halved lengthwise and thinly sliced crosswise

1/2 pound (225 g) stale country-style bread, cut into 3/4-inch cubes

About 6 cups (1470 ml) hot vegetable or chicken stock

2 cups (475 ml) Chianti or other light-bodied red wine

1 teaspoon (5 ml) salt

1/2 (2 ml) teaspoon freshly ground black pepper

Freshly grated parmesan cheese

*This rustic, hearty soup is a fine way to use wonderful but stale country-style bread with a dense crumb and a leftover half-bottle of good wine that you couldn't finish or bear to throw out. You may omit the wine and use all stock, but the wine does contribute a pleasant counterpoint to the sweet onions. If you don't have stale bread, spread cut bread on baking sheets and dry it at 300°F (150°C) oven for 15 minutes.*

In a large heavy-bottomed nonreactive soup pot, combine the butter and oil and heat over medium heat. Add half the onions and sauté them for 3 minutes, stirring occasionally. Add the remaining onions, toss well, stir, and sauté 2 to 3 minutes longer. Reduce the heat to medium low, stir, cover, and cook for 15 minutes, stirring occasionally so that the onions don't stick. The onions should just start to become golden brown.

Add the bread to the onions, stir well, cover, and cook for 2 minutes. Add the stock, wine, salt, and pepper, stir well, and cook 10 to 15 minutes. In batches, puree half the soup in a blender or processor and return it to the pot. Stir well and cook for 5 minutes longer. Thin with additional stock if desired.

Adjust the seasoning. Serve hot garnished with parmesan cheese.

# Sauté of Leeks, Endive, and Radicchio with Linguine

*The flavors of this combination of sweet and bitter vegetables mellow when it is served over pasta. We also like to serve the sauté with baked fish, chicken, or ham, and as a topping for pizza or focaccia.*

1 ½ pounds (675 g) leeks

8 ounces (225 g) Belgian endive: 2 medium heads

6 ounces (170 g) radicchio: 1 medium head

3 tablespoons (45 ml) extra-virgin olive oil

Salt and freshly ground pepper

About 1 tablespoon (15 ml) balsamic vinegar

12 ounces (340 g) fresh linguine noodles

Freshly grated parmesan cheese

Put a large nonreactive pot of water on to boil for the pasta.

Wash the leeks well, trim the roots and tops, leaving 2 inches (5 cm) of green. Halve the leeks lengthwise, rinse again if necessary, and pat them dry. Slice them crosswise into 1/4-inch (5-mm) slices.

Rinse the endive and radicchio and remove the outer leaves if necessary. Cut the endive crosswise into 1/4-inch (5-mm) slices. Halve the radicchio lengthwise and cut it crosswise into 1/4-inch (5-mm) slices.

Heat 2 tablespoons (30 ml) oil in a large sauté pan over medium heat. Add the leeks and sauté them, stirring occasionally, for 5 minutes. Add the pasta to the boiling water to cook so that it will be ready as soon as the vegetables are done.

Add the endive to the leeks, stir for 1 minute, and cover the pan. Cook 3 minutes, stirring once. Add the radicchio, salt and pepper to taste, stir well, cover the pan, and cook for 3 minutes.

When the pasta is al dente, drain it, reserving 1/4 cup (60 ml) of the water, and add it to the sautéed vegetables with the reserved water. Add the remaining oil and the vinegar and toss well. Reduce the heat to low and cover the pan for 1 minute. Adjust the seasoning with salt, pepper, a little more olive oil, or balsamic vinegar. Serve hot garnished with parmesan cheese.

# ONION AND NOODLE KUGEL WITH HERBS

Serves 8 to 10 as a first course or
side dish, 4 to 6 as a main dish

*This simple, savory kugel makes a fine first course, perhaps followed by lemony fish fillets or chicken breasts and a salad. As a supper or luncheon main dish, all it needs is country rye bread and a salad. It is excellent as a side dish with roast beef, pork, ham, or chicken. If you are watching your fat intake, use low- or nonfat milk and cottage cheese or ricotta.*

1 pound (450 g) wide egg noodles
2 tablespoons (30 ml) extra-virgin olive oil
1 tablespoon (15 ml) unsalted butter
1 pound (450 g) yellow onions, peeled, quartered lengthwise, and cut crosswise 1/4 inch (5 mm) thick
2 cups (475 ml) milk
1 cup (240 ml) small-curd cottage or ricotta cheese
2 extra-large eggs, lightly beaten
1 teaspoon (5 ml) salt
1/2 teaspoon (2 ml) freshly ground pepper

1/3 cup (80 ml) and 2 tablespoons (30 ml) freshly grated parmesan cheese
1½ teaspoons (8 ml) paprika
Cayenne pepper to taste
2 teaspoons (5 ml) minced fresh marjoram or thyme, or 3/4 teaspoon (4 ml) dried, crumbled
1/2 cup (120 ml) Italian parsley, chopped
2 tablespoons (30 ml) snipped fresh chives
Generous 1/2 cup (120 ml) dried bread crumbs

Cook the noodles al dente, toss them with 1 tablespoon (15 ml) olive oil, and season with salt and pepper.

Preheat the oven to 375°F (190°C). Butter a 2-quart (2-l) gratin dish.

In a large sauté pan, heat the butter and remaining olive oil over medium heat. Add the onions and sauté, stirring occasionally, for 10 minutes. Meanwhile, place the milk, cottage cheese, eggs, salt, pepper, 1/3 cup (80 ml) parmesan cheese, 1/2 teaspoon paprika, cayenne, marjoram or thyme, parsley, and chives in a large bowl and mix well.

Stir in the cooked noodles and the sautéed onions. Transfer the mixture to the prepared gratin dish and sprinkle it with about a teaspoon paprika. Toss the bread crumbs with the remaining parmesan cheese and sprinkle the mixture over the top of the kugel.

Bake the kugel for 15 minutes, reduce the heat to 325°F (160°C) and bake 25 minutes longer. Remove from the oven and serve hot.

# MAIN COURSES

*Mussels with Shallots, Onions, and Thyme*

Serves 4 to 8

## Pie Shell

1½ cups (360 ml) all-purpose flour

1/2 teaspoon (2 ml) salt

6 tablespoons (90 ml) unsalted butter, cut in bits

3 tablespoons (45 ml) vegetable shortening

4 to 6 tablespoons (60 to 90 ml) ice water

1½ teaspoons (8 ml) lemon juice or vinegar

Mix the flour with the salt in a bowl or food processor. Cut the butter and shortening into the flour. Mix 4 tablespoons (60 ml) ice water with the lemon juice or vinegar and add it to the flour mixture. Mix just enough to bind the dough, sprinkling in more ice water if needed.

Gather the dough and shape it in a flattened round or square, cover, and chill it at least 30 minutes. Roll the dough to fit a 9-inch (23-cm) pie plate or tart pan with removable bottom at least 1 inch (2 cm) deep. The dough should be thick, about 3/16 inch (4 mm). Cover and chill for at least an hour.

When ready to bake the shell, preheat the oven to 400°F (200°C). Prick the shell and line it with aluminum foil. Fill the foil with dried beans or pie weights. Bake the shell for 15 minutes, then remove the foil and weights. Bake the shell 7 minutes longer, or until it is pale golden brown. Remove it to a rack and cool to room temperature. If you are baking the shell a day ahead, wrap the pie plate and shell completely with aluminum foil after it has cooled.

*Sweet onions and vine-ripe tomatoes are high on our list of quintessential summer foods. This dish combines them for a first course, brunch, lunch, or light supper dish, or an accompaniment to simple grills. The delicate custard and juiciness of the tomatoes contrast superbly with the flaky, toothsome crust. The pie is best served just warm or at room temperature. A square tart pan makes a nice presentation. We like to bake the pie shell in the cool of the evening the day before we plan to serve the pie. A good variation is to use thin slices of zucchini, about 1/8 inch (2 mm), rather than tomato slices; place them on the custard after sprinkling on the cheese and bake the pie until the custard is set.*

*Another variation is to use marjoram or oregano instead of basil.*

## Filling

1 pound (450 g) sweet onions, halved lengthwise and thinly sliced crosswise

2 tablespoons (30 ml) olive oil

Handful of sweet basil leaves

2 extra-large eggs

About 1 cup (240 ml) milk

Salt and freshly ground pepper

1/2 cup (120 ml) grated gruyère or emmenthal cheese

1½ pounds (647 g) firm-ripe tomatoes

Basil sprigs for garnish, optional

Preheat the oven to 375°F (190°C).

Soften the onions in the oil in a sauté pan over medium heat for 10 minutes, or until they are crisp-tender and pale golden. Transfer them to a bowl to cool. Shred the basil leaves. Season the onions well with salt and pepper and toss them with the basil.

Beat the eggs lightly in a 2-cup (475 ml) measuring cup and add milk to come to the 1½-cup (360-ml) mark. Season lightly.

Sprinkle half the cheese over the bottom of the baked pie shell. Lay the onions over the cheese. Pour the custard mixture over the onions and sprinkle it with the remaining cheese.

Bake the pie for 25 minutes. Meanwhile, slice the tomatoes at least 1/2 inch (1 cm) thick. Place them on the pie and bake 10 minutes longer, or until the custard is set.

Cool the pie on a rack for at least 30 minutes before cutting and serving. You may brush the tops of the tomatoes with a little olive oil and garnish the pie with basil sprigs.

# SOUTHWESTERN GRITS, ONION, AND CHILE CASSEROLE

5 cups (1200 ml) water
1¼ (300 ml) cups grits
1/2 teaspoon (2 ml) salt
1 tablespoon (15 ml) olive or
   vegetable oil
1 to 2 large yellow or white onions,
   quartered lengthwise and sliced
   3/8-inch thick, about 4 cups
   (950 ml) sliced
1 cup (240 ml) milk
3 extra-large eggs
1 teaspoon (5 ml) dried thyme,
   crumbled

1/2 teaspoon (2 ml) Hungarian
   paprika
4 or 5 dashes Tabasco
Salt and freshly ground pepper
1½ cups (360 ml) grated sharp
   cheddar cheese
6 Anaheim or New Mexico green
   chiles, roasted, peeled, seeded, and
   cut into strips
15-ounce (420-g) can tomatoes, cut
   into large dice

*You can assemble this casserole in half an hour and put it in the oven an hour before dinner. It's easy, homey, satisfying, stick-to-your-ribs food, good even when made with reduced-fat milk. If you don't like hot peppers, use mild ones or leave them out.*

Combine the water, grits, and salt in a heavy-bottomed pan and bring to a boil over medium-high heat. Reduce the heat to medium low and cook, stirring occasionally, for about 20 minutes, or until the grits are barely tender.

Meanwhile, heat the oil in a large sauté pan over medium heat and sauté the onions for 15 minutes, or until golden brown. Preheat oven to 375°F (190°C) and butter a 2-quart (2-l) casserole.

In a medium bowl, combine the milk, eggs, thyme, paprika, Tabasco, salt, and pepper, and stir well with a fork. Stir in 1 cup (240 ml) of the cheese.

In a large bowl, combine the grits, onions, chiles, and tomatoes, and toss well. Stir in the milk mixture. Transfer the mixture to the casserole and spread it evenly; sprinkle it with the remaining cheese. Bake 45 to 50 minutes. Remove the casserole from the oven, let stand for 5 minutes, and serve hot.

# POLENTA WITH ONIONS, SPINACH, AND BLUE CHEESE

Serves 4 as a main course,
6 as a side dish or appetizer

## Polenta

6 cups (1420 ml) water

1 ½ (8 ml) teaspoons salt

1 ½ cups (360 ml) medium- or
coarse-grain polenta

Bring the water to a boil in a large nonreactive pot, then add the salt. Slowly pour the polenta into the boiling water in a steady stream, stirring continuously. When the mixture begins to bubble and erupt, reduce the heat to low so that it doesn't spatter out of the pot. Cook the polenta, stirring frequently so that it doesn't stick, for 35 to 40 minutes. The polenta should be thick.

Pour the polenta into a lightly oiled loaf pan and let it cool. Turn the polenta out onto a board and slice it 5/8 inch (1 cm) thick, then cut it into 2-inch (5-cm) squares. Lightly brush the squares with olive oil and place them on a baking sheet under the broiler, on a griddle over medium heat, or on a grill over a medium-hot fire. Cook the polenta for 3 to 5 minutes on each side, or until it is golden brown on the edges.

Preheat the oven to 375°F (190°C). Lightly oil a 9-by-13-inch (23-by-33-cm) casserole or gratin dish.

*This dish brings memories of fall and winter evenings in Tuscany, when friends would drop by after a walk in the country and we would make a warming dinner from the staples that we had on hand. Polenta, a cold-weather favorite, can be made in advance and reheated while the onions are cooking for the topping. Assembling and baking the dish takes less than half an hour. Of course, you can make the whole dish on Italian time, chatting with friends, roasting and nibbling chestnuts, sipping red wine, taking turns stirring the polenta and judging its doneness. We can't really say how long this is.*

## Topping

2 tablespoons (30 ml) extra-virgin
    olive oil
1 pound (450 g) onions, quartered
    lengthwise and sliced crosswise
1 generous quart (1 l) small spinach
    leaves without stems, washed

2 teaspoons (10 ml) fresh oregano,
    chopped
6 ounces (180 g) taleggio or soft
    blue cheese, diced
Salt and freshly ground pepper

Heat the olive oil in a large sauté pan over medium-low heat. Add the onions and sauté them for 10 minutes, stirring occasionally. Add the oregano, stir, and sauté for 5 minutes longer, or until the onions are golden.

Layer half the polenta squares in the prepared dish. Cover them with spinach leaves and then cover the spinach with half the onions. Salt and pepper generously. Scatter half the cheese over the onions. Layer the rest of the polenta, onions, salt and pepper, and cheese. Bake in a hot oven 15 minutes, or until the cheese is melted and the dish is heated through. Serve immediately.

# Rice with Leeks and Mushrooms

2 cups (475 ml) white or brown
   rice
4 1/2 to 5 cups (1070 to 1200 ml)
   hot vegetable or defatted chicken
   stock or water
1 teaspoon ( 5 ml) salt
2 tablespoons (30 ml) olive oil

1 tablespoon (15 ml) unsalted butter
4 leeks, split lengthwise, rinsed well,
   and sliced crosswise 1/4 inch (5
   mm) thick
2 cups (475 ml) sliced mushrooms
Salt and freshly ground pepper

*This simple, hearty dish is delicious served with grilled or roasted game, meat, or poultry, or as a vegetarian main course. Sometimes we substitute wild rice for half the regular, cooking it separately, and for a special treat, we use chanterelles or morels. Often we add a little red or white wine in place of the stock at the end of cooking.*

Combine the rice, 4 cups (950 ml) stock or water, and salt in a nonreactive, heavy-bottomed saucepan. Cover and bring to a boil over medium-high heat. Reduce the heat to medium low. Cook white rice about 25 minutes and brown rice for 45 minutes, or until tender but al dente.

Meanwhile, heat the olive oil and butter over medium heat in a large nonstick skillet. Add the leeks and sauté them about 3 minutes, stirring occasionally. Add the mushrooms, toss them with the leeks, and sauté them about 3 minutes, stirring occasionally. Add about 1/4 to 1/2 cup (60 to 80 ml) of the remaining stock and salt and pepper to taste. Reduce the heat to medium low, cover, and cook about 5 minutes longer, stirring occasionally.

When the rice is done, transfer it to the pan of vegetables and toss well over medium-low heat. Add the remaining stock if necessary and adjust the seasoning. Serve hot.

# MUSSELS WITH SHALLOTS, ONIONS, AND THYME

Serves 4 to 6

*The French have championed the combination of shallots with fish and shellfish, leaving the use of other alliums with seafood to their Mediterranean neighbors, the Italians and Spanish. This dish unites elements from all those cuisines—shallots, onions, wine, and saffron. Serve lots of crusty bread to soak up the flavorful, fragrant juices. Mussel lovers can happily make a meal of the dish with bread and a salad, or it may be served as a first course.*

*1 medium onion, diced*
*4 large shallots, finely diced*
*2 tablespoons (30 ml) olive oil*
*4 pounds (1.8 kg) mussels*
*8 thyme sprigs*
*1 cup (240 ml) dry white wine*

*2 cups (475 ml) fish broth or bottled clam juice*
*1 small pinch saffron*
*Freshly ground black pepper*
*Chopped Italian parsley for garnish*

Cook the onion and half the shallots in the olive oil in a sauté pan over medium heat for 5 minutes, or until they soften.

Debeard and scrub the mussels. Place them in a nonreactive pan with the remaining shallots, thyme, wine, and fish broth. Cover and place over high heat. Cook 3 minutes, or just until the mussels open. Remove the mussels to a bowl.

Strain the broth through rinsed fine-weave cheesecloth or paper towels into the pan with the onions and shallots. Add the saffron and simmer the mixture 5 minutes. Season with freshly ground black pepper.

Add the mussels to the broth and heat through. Serve hot in warm bowls, garnished with chopped parsley.

# ROAST CHICKEN STUFFED WITH LEEKS, SHALLOTS, AND TARRAGON

Serves 6 to 8

1 6-pound (2.7-kg) roasting chicken
1 lemon
2 pounds (1 kg) leeks, white and tender green part only, halved lengthwise, rinsed well, and thinly sliced crosswise
4 large shallots, halved lengthwise and thinly sliced crosswise
3 garlic cloves, minced
3 tablespoons (45 ml) unsalted butter
1½ cups (360 ml) fresh bread crumbs
4 tarragon sprigs, leaves chopped, or 1/2 teaspoon (2 ml) dried leaves
Salt and freshly ground pepper
Tarragon sprigs for garnish, optional

*Many of the onion family have an affinity for tarragon, as does chicken. Here we have combined leeks, shallots, and tarragon in a stuffing with just enough bread to bind it together. The result has won superlatives from those who love stuffing as well as those who usually don't eat it.*

Rinse the chicken well and pat dry. Remove the excess fat and reserve the giblets for another use. Remove the zest from the lemon and chop it finely; reserve for the stuffing. Salt and pepper the chicken well and rub it with lemon juice.

Over low heat, soften the leeks, shallots, and garlic in the butter in a nonreactive sauté pan, covered. Remove the vegetables to a bowl to cool. Add the reserved lemon zest, bread crumbs, and tarragon. Season well with salt and pepper.

Preheat the oven to 450°F (230°C). Loosen the skin over the breast and stuff the space with about half the stuffing. Spoon the remaining stuffing into the cavity. Place the chicken, breast up, on a rack in a roasting pan. Roast it for 30 minutes, then reduce heat to 370°F (190°C) and roast an hour longer, or until the juices run clear when you pierce the thick part of a thigh. Cover the chicken loosely with foil if it is browning too rapidly.

Let the chicken stand at room temperature for at least 15 minutes before carving. Carve the chicken, slicing the breasts on a diagonal into four pieces and dividing the thighs and drumsticks into two portions each. Place the chicken pieces on a serving platter with the stuffing in the center. Garnish with fresh tarragon sprigs, if desired.

# Steak Smothered with Balsamic Onions

4 New York or other strip steaks,
   1½ inches (4 cm) thick
4 tablespoons (60 ml) balsamic
   vinegar
2 tablespoons (30 ml) olive oil
1 teaspoon (5 ml) fresh thyme leaves,
   or 1/2 teaspoon (2 ml) dried
Salt and freshly ground pepper

2 tablespoons (30 ml) unsalted
   butter
2 pounds (900 g) Red Torpedo or
   other sweet-tasting onions, halved
   lengthwise and thinly sliced
   crosswise or slivered lengthwise
1 cup (240 ml) beef or chicken stock

*This way of preparing the onions—adding the thyme while they are caramelizing and using vegetable or chicken stock, depending what you would like to serve with them—makes an excellent accompaniment to mashed potatoes and simple chicken and fish dishes as well as to steak. The dish is also delicious with a pound (450 g) of shallots in place of the onions. You may cook the steaks on a grill, reserving the marinade. Let the steaks rest on a platter for 5 to 10 minutes. Pour any juices from the meat, along with the marinade, stock, and remaining balsamic vinegar into the onion pan and finish as described below.*

Trim the steaks of excess fat. Mix 1 tablespoon (15 ml) balsamic vinegar with the olive oil and thyme. Rub the steaks with the mixture. Marinate the steaks in a single layer for an hour or two at cool room temperature or as long as twelve hours in the refrigerator. Bring the steaks to cool room temperature before cooking them.

Melt the butter in a nonreactive sauté pan over medium heat. Stir in the onions to coat them well. Add 2 tablespoons (30 ml) of balsamic vinegar. Stew the onions, covered, stirring occasionally, 25 minutes, or until they are soft and slightly caramelized. Season with salt and pepper.

Meanwhile, heat a large heavy sauté pan or ridged grill pan over medium-high heat. Salt and pepper the steaks and place them in the pan. Reduce the heat to medium and cook the steaks 4 to 6 minutes on each side, or until medium-rare. Remove the steaks to a warm platter to rest while you finish the sauce.

Deglaze the steak pan with the stock, scraping well. When the onions are done, place them on the steaks. Pour the deglazing juices and the remaining vinegar into the onion pan and cook over high heat for 2 or 3 minutes to reduce the liquid by about half. Pour the sauce over the onions and steak and serve immediately.

# VEGETABLES AND SALADS

*Orange and Onion Salad*

# Baked Onions, Southern Italian Style

Serves 6

In most regions of Italy, baked onions, stuffed or whole, are served as vegetables or cut into sections to include on antipasto platters. They also make a good main course preceded by a soup and followed by a salad. This dish is inspired by the flavors of southern Italy: olive oil, anchovies, and the sweet and sour of currants or raisins, wine, vinegar, and capers. If you don't care for anchovies, you may substituted 3 ounces (85 g) finely diced baked ham, prosciutto, or lamb, or 3 ounces (85 g) pancetta, finely diced and rendered crisp. For a meatless version, substitute Kalamata olives for the anchovies and chop a bit more of the onion centers.

6 medium white onions, 2 to 2½ pounds (1.1 kg)
6 whole salt-pack anchovies, or 12 anchovy fillets
1/2 cup (120 ml) fine dry bread crumbs
1/4 cup (60 ml) extra-virgin olive oil
1/4 cup (60 ml) currants or raisins

3 sprigs fresh thyme, or 1 teaspoon (5 ml) dried leaves
3 tablespoons (45 ml) imported dry Marsala
1 tablespoon (15 ml) white wine vinegar
Salt and freshly ground pepper
1 tablespoon (15 ml) small capers

Skin the onions. Trim a little from the root ends so that the onions will sit flat in a baking dish and cut an X in the root ends. Place the onions in a large pot of lightly salted boiling water and cook them 15 minutes. Rinse under cold water. Slice 1/2 inch (1 cm) from the top of each onion and discard. Remove the centers, leaving at least four layers of onion to hold the filling, and place the onions upside down to drain. Reserve the centers.

Rinse and bone the salt-pack anchovies, if you are using them. Finely chop the anchovy fillets and half the reserved onion centers and mix them in a bowl. Reserve the remaining centers for another use.

Preheat the oven to 375°F (190°C).

Heat 3 tablespoons (45 ml) olive oil over medium heat until the oil shimmers. Add the bread crumbs and sauté until they are light golden brown. Stir in the currants or raisins. Season with salt and pepper.

Fill the onion shells with the stuffing and place them in a baking dish that just holds them comfortably. Drizzle with the remaining olive oil. Break the thyme sprigs into pieces and scatter them or sprinkle the dried thyme over the onions. Sprinkle the onions with Marsala and vinegar, and salt and pepper lightly.

Cover the dish tightly and bake 40 minutes at 375°F (190°C). Remove the cover and baste the onions with the pan juices. Bake 15 minutes longer, or until the onions are tender but still hold their shape. Serve hot or at room temperature. Just before serving, scatter the capers over the onions.

# Roasted Onions, Artichokes, and Potatoes

Serves 4 to 6

*This dish was inspired by a dish of roast potatoes and artichokes that we first enjoyed when we lived in Italy in the 1970s as well as by Paul Bertolli's Potatoes and Onions Roasted in Vinegar and Thyme from* **Chez Panisse Cooking** *(Random House, 1988). It accompanies roasts and braises well; in winter, we often serve it with* Chicken with 40 Cloves of Garlic from **The Garlic Book** *(Interweave Press, 1993). We also love it as a spring main course preceded by watercress soup and followed by a salad.*

1 pound (450 g) pearl, boiling
    onions, or cipolline
2 1/2 pounds (1.1 kg) artichokes
1 lemon
2 pounds (900 g) russet potatoes
Salt and freshly ground pepper

5 sprigs tarragon
1/4 cup (60 ml) balsamic vinegar
1/4 cup (60 ml) dry white wine
1/4 cup (60 ml) extra-virgin olive
    oil

Parboil the onions for 5 minutes in at least 2 quarts (2 l) of water. Drain and rinse them under cold water. Trim the root and stem ends, and remove the skins and the outer layer of flesh. Reserve the onions.

Trim the artichokes to the hearts and remove the chokes, rubbing the flesh with a cut lemon as you trim. Cut each artichoke heart into six or eight wedges, depending on the size of the artichokes. Place the wedges in a bowl of cold water with the juice of half a lemon to cover.

Scrub the potatoes well. Quarter them lengthwise, then cut each quarter crosswise into eight pieces. Preheat the oven to 400°F (200°C).

Place the onions, artichokes, and potatoes in a 3-quart (3-l) baking dish. Season well with salt and pepper and toss. Bury the tarragon sprigs among the vegetables. Drizzle with the vinegar, wine, and oil.

Cover the dish with aluminum foil and place it in the oven. Roast for 1 hour, turning the vegetables three times to coat well, and replacing the foil after turning. Serve hot, warm, or at room temperature.

# WINE AND VINEGAR GLAZED ONIONS

10 ounces (280 g) pearl or other
    small onions
1 tablespoon (15 ml) unsalted butter
1 tablespoon (15 ml) olive oil
4 tablespoons (60 ml) Chianti or red
    wine

1 tablespoon (15 ml) balsamic or red
    wine vinegar
Salt
Freshly ground pepper

*These simple little glazed onions taste best when served with other simple dishes such as oven-roasted or sautéed potatoes, sautéed Sugar Snap peas or braised English peas, roast or grilled lamb, or salmon. The recipe is easily doubled.*

Drop the onions in a pot of boiling water and simmer 3 minutes. Drain well and cool under cold water. Drain the onions, trim the root ends, and peel them. Pat them dry on paper towels.

In a sauté pan that will hold all the onions in one layer, melt the butter over medium heat. Add the oil.

Add the onions and sauté them 2 to 3 minutes, shaking the pan occasionally. Turn the onions when they are golden brown on one side and sauté 2 to 3 minutes longer. Add the wine and cook, shaking the pan, for 4 minutes, or until the wine is nearly gone.

Add the vinegar and cook until it is almost gone, shaking the pan occasionally. Salt and pepper to taste. Serve hot.

# Sauerkraut with Onions

*Ordinary sauerkraut gains a bit of character with this treatment. Susan's Irish grandmother always put a turkey neck with the onions in the sauerkraut pot and let the mixture cook over low heat on the back of the stove while she prepared the rest of the dinner. Fresh sauerkraut packed in plastic bags in the meat department of the supermarket or sauerkraut packed in glass jars has the best flavor. We like this kraut with mashed potatoes and gravy and roast poultry. Leftovers keep well in the refrigerator for a week and are perfect for Reuben sandwiches.*

1 large yellow or white onion
1½ tablespoons (22 ml) unsalted butter
1½ to 2 pounds (675 to 900 g) fresh sauerkraut

1 teaspoon (5 ml) bruised caraway seed
6 juniper berries
1 cup (240 ml) white wine, dry but a little fruity

Peel the onion, quarter it lengthwise, and thinly slice the quarters crosswise. Melt the butter over medium heat in a large nonreactive sauté pan. Sauté the onion over medium low heat for about 10 minutes, stirring occasionally.

Drain the excess liquid from the sauerkraut and add it to the onions. Add the caraway seeds and juniper berries and stir well. Add the wine, stir, cover, leaving the lid slightly ajar, and simmer 20 minutes. Reduce the heat if the sauerkraut is simmering and the wine is evaporating. Add a little more wine if necessary, stir, and adjust the seasoning. Remove the juniper berries.

The sauerkraut may be held over low heat for 20 minutes or so, or it may be reheated before serving. Serve hot.

# LEEK AND CELERY ROOT GRATIN WITH HORSERADISH

2 pounds (900 g) leeks
1 pound (450 g) celery root
1 tablespoon (15 ml) unsalted butter
1 1/2 tablespoons (22 ml) extra-
   virgin olive oil
Salt and freshly ground pepper

1 cup (240 ml) stale bread, cut into
   1/4-inch (5-mm) dice
1 garlic clove, minced
1/2 cup (120 ml) whipping cream
2 tablespoons (30 ml) prepared
   horseradish, or 1 1/2 tablespoons
   (22 ml) freshly grated horseradish

*In this plain, yet refined dish, the earthy, celerylike flavor of celeriac complements the sweetness of leeks. The horseradish remains quietly pungent, but its heat disappears when it is cooked. It is excellent with roast duck, game birds, chicken, and beef. We sometimes make a meal of it, accompanied by pumpernickel or rye bread, radishes, pickled onions, and some aged cheshire, cheddar, or gouda.*

Clean and trim the leeks, leaving about 2 inches (5 cm) of pale tender green, then halve them lengthwise. Rinse well and pat them dry. Slice them crosswise 1/4 inch (5 mm) thick.

Peel the celery root, cut it into eight wedges lengthwise, and slice the wedges crosswise 1/4 inch (5 mm) thick.

Preheat the oven to 350°F (180°C). Butter a 1 1/2-quart (1 1/2 -l) gratin dish.

Heat the butter and 1 tablespoon (15 ml) oil in a large sauté pan over medium heat and add the celery root. Cook and stir for 4 minutes. Add the leeks and cook and stir for 6 minutes longer. Season with salt and pepper and transfer the sautéed vegetables to the gratin dish.

Add the remaining oil to the hot sauté pan along with the bread and garlic. Add salt and pepper and toss over medium heat for 4 minutes. Remove the pan from the heat.

Stir the cream and horseradish together and drizzle over the sautéed vegetables. Sprinkle the bread on top. Bake for 25 minutes, or until golden and bubbling. Serve hot.

# ONION AND CUCUMBER SALAD

*Variations on this recipe have been made for centuries in Central, Eastern, and Northern Europe. We like to use red onions for color contrast and rice vinegar for a lighter taste. If your onion is pungent, rinse it well after slicing it. You may add a little fresh chopped tarragon or dill, but the dish is good just as is. The texture of the salad is crispest when it is prepared no more than two hours in advance.*

About 1 pound (450 g) cucumbers
1/2 large red onion
3 tablespoons (45 ml) extra-virgin olive oil

About 3 tablespoons (45 ml) rice vinegar
Pinch sugar
Salt and freshly ground pepper

Peel the cucumbers if they are not home-grown. Slice them thinly. Cut the onion in half lengthwise and thinly slice it crosswise. Combine the cucumbers and onion in a bowl. Add 3 tablespoons (45 ml) olive oil, the vinegar, and sugar, and season with salt and pepper. Toss well.

Let the salad stand 20 to 30 minutes. Stir well and adjust the seasoning; add a little more oil or vinegar if necessary. Cover and refrigerate the salad if you are preparing it in advance. Serve at cool room temperature.

# POTATO SALAD WITH SCALLIONS AND RED PEPPERS

8 servings

2 1/4 pounds (1 kg) red-skinned or gold-fleshed potatoes, cut into bite-sized pieces

About 3 tablespoons (45 ml) fresh lemon juice

About 4 tablespoons (60 ml) extra-virgin olive oil

Salt and freshly ground black pepper

1 large or 2 medium red or yellow bell peppers

2 bunches scallions, trimmed to 2 inches (5 cm) of green and thinly sliced

1/4 cup (60 ml) coarsely chopped fresh basil leaves

2 hard-cooked eggs, coarsely diced

*This potato salad without mayonnaise was inspired by a recipe for Warm Potato Salad with Fried Red Peppers from* Home Cooking *by Laurie Colwin, Alfred A. Knopf, Inc., 1988). It is simple to make and may be prepared in advance; we like it best served at cool room temperature. Vary it by adding your favorite herb or other vegetables, such as artichoke hearts, or by replacing the lemon juice with white wine vinegar. We like to use Yukon Gold, Red Bliss, or German Fingerling potatoes, but any waxy potato will do; scrub the potatoes and leave the peels on or peel them, as you like.*

In a large pan, steam the potatoes over boiling water, covered, for 15 minutes, or until tender yet firm.

Meanwhile, combine the lemon juice and 2 tablespoons (30 ml) oil in a small bowl, and salt and pepper generously; stir well with a fork.

Stem and seed the peppers and cut them into strips about 1 1/2 inches (4 cm) long and 3/8 inch (8 mm) wide. Heat the remaining oil in a sauté pan over medium heat and sauté the peppers for 7 minutes, stirring occasionally. Or roast the peppers over a flame or under the broiler. When the skins are somewhat loose and blackened, remove the peppers to a paper bag. When the peppers are cool enough to handle, peel, stem, and seed them and cut them into strips.

Drain the potatoes, and toss them with the peppers, scallions, basil, and vinaigrette. Add the remaining oil if you roasted the peppers. Season with salt and pepper. Add the eggs, stir well, and adjust the seasoning. Let cool to room temperature. Serve the salad at room temperature or slightly chilled.

# Orange and Onion Salad

Serves 8

This salad is juicy, refreshing, and full of flavor. Any type of onion may be used; we like red for its pretty color. Some prefer the contrast of a pungent onion, but we usually make this salad with a sweet one. Garnacha tinto vinegar, made from a Catalan wine grape, has an unusual woody flavor that adds a nice dimension to the dish, but sherry and red wine vinegar work well. Orange and onion salads are served around the Mediterranean, particularly in North Africa, Sicily, and Spain, and in the Middle East. The recipe can be easily halved.

1 small red onion, about 5 ounces (140 g)
1/3 cup (80 ml) fresh-squeezed orange juice
1 tablespoon (15 ml) garnacha tinto, sherry, or red wine vinegar
1/2 cup (120 ml) extra-virgin

olive oil
Scant 1/2 teaspoon (2 ml) salt
Freshly ground black pepper
1 garlic clove
4 large oranges, peeled and seeded
1/3 cup (80 ml) pitted Kalamata olives, thinly sliced

Cut the onion crosswise into thin slices and place them in a bowl of cold water for about 10 minutes.

In a jar with a lid, combine the orange juice, vinegar, oil, salt, and pepper. Press the garlic into the jar and shake vigorously to combine the ingredients.

Slice the oranges 3/8 inch (8 mm) thick and arrange them on a platter. Drain the onion slices and scatter them over the oranges. Sprinkle the olives over the salad. Shake the vinaigrette, pour it over the salad, and serve at room temperature. The salad may be prepared in advance, covered, and refrigerated. Bring the salad to cool room temperature and dress just before serving.

# SAUCES, ACCOMPANIMENTS, AND CONDIMENTS

*Grilled Onions*

# ONION MUSHROOM GRAVY

Makes about 3 1/2 cups (830 ml)

*Here is a quick, versatile gravy that calls for neither meat stock nor juices. It may be made with either fresh mushrooms or with dried porcini, cêpes, or shiitake. You will need about a tablespoon (15 ml) less fat when using the dried mushrooms. Soak 1/2 ounce (15 g) dried mushrooms in 3/4 cup (180 ml) boiling water for about 20 minutes. Rinse them well and strain the soaking liquid, making sure it contains no grit. Cut the mushrooms into small pieces and add them along with their liquid when you add the last liquid to the gravy.*

1 pound (450 g) onions, diced
4 sprigs thyme, or 1/2 teaspoon (2 ml) dried thyme, crumbled
3 tablespoons (45 ml) unsalted butter or extra-virgin olive oil
1/2 pound (225 g) mushrooms, sliced 1/4 inch (5 mm) thick
Salt
3 tablespoons (45 ml) flour

2 1/2 cups (590 ml) milk or chicken broth
2 teaspoons (10 ml) miso paste, or soy sauce
Freshly ground pepper, or cayenne pepper
Dash or two Angostura bitters

Melt the butter in a large, nonreactive skillet over medium heat. Soften the onions with the thyme about 15 minutes, or until they are golden brown. Add the mushrooms, season lightly with salt, and increase the heat. Cook the mixture about 10 minutes, or until the mushrooms give up their juices, stirring or tossing occasionally. Remove the thyme sprigs.

Sprinkle the vegetables with the flour, stir well and cook 3 to 4 minutes longer. If you are using soft miso, add it with 1/2 cup (120 ml) milk or broth and stir well to dissolve the miso. If you have dry miso, crumble it into the pan and add 1 cup (240 ml) of milk or broth and stir well to dissolve it. Add the remaining liquid and cook about 10 minutes over medium-low heat, stirring occasionally. Adjust the seasoning with freshly ground black or cayenne pepper, bitters, and salt.

The recipe is quite adaptable to the exigencies of your pantry and refrigerator. We have made it with cultivated and wild mushrooms (the latter being especially tasty with wild rice), fresh and dried thyme, butter/or oil or a combination, milk, homemade chicken broth and nonfat low-sodium canned chicken broth, miso and soy sauce. If you can find the miso, available in most Oriental and health food stores, it adds a special flavor, but soy sauce works well.

# Shallot Vinaigrette

*Use this vinaigrette in place of tartar sauce with fish. It is wonderful in salmon salads, adds a nice allium crunch to simple green salads, and is especially tasty in potato and lentil salads. We like an unusual coleslaw of cabbage, fresh fennel, and red bell peppers with shallot vinaigrette. Use roasted shallots (page 88) for salads with bittersweet greens such as radicchio and Belgian or curly endive, and add 1 teaspoon (5 ml) balsamic vinegar. You may sub-stitute an equal quantity of parsley for the chervil or dill, or about half as much chopped tarragon.*

*The addition of 1 teaspoon (5 ml) dijon-style mustard stirred in before adding the olive oil is good in hearty salads.*

2 shallots, finely diced
3 tablespoons (45 ml) chopped fresh chervil or dill
5 to 6 tablespoons (75 to 90 ml)
sherry vinegar
2/3 cup (160 ml) extra-virgin olive oil
Salt and freshly ground pepper

Place the shallots and chopped herbs in a small bowl. Stir in the vinegar. Whisk in the olive oil to make an emulsion. Season with salt and pepper. Adjust the seasoning with more vinegar, olive oil, salt, or pepper.

# GREEN ONION VINAIGRETTE

1 bunch green onions or scallions, trimmed with about 3 inches (8 cm) green

2 tablespoons (30 ml) white wine or tarragon vinegar

1/3 cup (80 ml) extra-virgin olive oil

3 sprigs fresh dill or tarragon, or vinegar-preserved tarragon, leaves removed

Salt and freshly ground pepper

Slice the scallions 1/4 inch (5 mm) thick. Place them in a blender or food processor along with the vinegar, oil, and herb leaves. Blend or process about 1 minute, or until the vinaigrette is emulsified.

Season the vinaigrette with salt and pepper and adjust with a few drops of vinegar or oil. Store, tightly covered, as long as 2 days in the refrigerator.

*In late winter and early spring, green onions are often inexpensive. This flavorful vinaigrette uses an entire bunch (usually six) in a dressing that is equally good with green or vegetable salads. Dill and tarragon both complement many winter vegetables such as beets, carrots, cauliflower, and potatoes. Half a cup (120 ml) of this vinaigrette is ample to dress 3 to 4 quarts (3 to 4 l) salad greens, or about 2 pounds (900 g) of vegetables.*

# Tunisian-Style Relish

*Donna Walters, a friend who lived in Tunisia, taught us to make this dish, which the Tunisians served as salad. It is more like a relish in North American cooking, and one that we always enjoy during the summer. It's equally good with rustic bread, pitas, or corn chips, and is a pleasant accompaniment to anything from the grill. Diced sweet onions may replace the scallions.*

*1 pound (450 g) ripe tomatoes*
*Salt and freshly ground pepper*
*2 bunches green onions or scallions*
*4 to 6 small, hot green chiles such as*
*serrano, fingerling, or green cayenne, about the same thickness as the scallions*
*2 teaspoons (10 ml) fresh lime juice*

Wash the tomatoes, onions, and chiles. Core the tomatoes, finely dice them, and place them in a bowl. Season them well with salt and pepper.

Trim the scallions, leaving 2 inches (5 cm) of green. Slice them thinly and add them to the tomatoes.

Remove the stems and most of the seeds from the chiles, leaving them whole if possible. Slice them into thin rings and transfer them to the bowl. Toss the ingredients well and add the lime juice. Stir and adjust the seasoning. Serve immediately or within 2 hours at room temperature.

# PICKLED ONIONS

2 ½ pounds (1.1 kg) Italian
  pickling onions, pearl onions, or
  boiling onions
3 cups (710 ml) white wine vinegar
3 cups (710 ml) water

3 tablespoons (45 ml) sugar
1 tablespoon (15 ml) kosher salt
1/3 cup (80 ml) olive oil
1/2 teaspoon (2 ml) black
  peppercorns

Bring a saucepan of water to a boil to blanch the onions. Combine 2¼ cups (540 ml) of the vinegar with 1½ cups (360 ml) water and the sugar in a 4-quart (4-l) or larger nonreactive pan and bring to a simmer.

Blanch the onions 2 minutes, rinse under cold water, and drain. Peel and trim the onions, beginning at the root ends. Add the onions to the vinegar-water solution, cover, and bring to a medium boil. Cook the onions 4 minutes.

To prepare the pickling liquid, bring the remaining vinegar, remaining water, salt, peppercorns, and olive oil to a boil in a small nonreactive pan. Reduce the heat and simmer 5 minutes.

With a slotted spoon or tongs, pack the onions in hot, sterilized pint canning jars. Divide the pickling liquid among the jars. Screw on hot, sterilized canning lids and rings. The pickles may be used immediately but are best after they have stood for a week. Store in a cool, dark place as long as 6 months. Store in the refrigerator after opening, and use within a week. Before serving refrigerated pickles, bring them to room temperature to liquify the olive oil.

*This common Italian pickling method is used for sweet peppers and mixed vegetable antipasto as well as onions. When Carolyn first learned it twenty-odd years ago in Tuscany, she was skeptical, then happily surprised that the vegetables kept so well and tasted so good, raised as she was on the keep-botulism-out-of-the-cupboard-by-water-bathing-pickles-a-good-long-time style of pickling. For the best flavor and texture, use freshly harvested onions: the onions should be very firm, and not sprouting. These pickled onions are as welcome on a platter of crudités as they are served with bread and olives, meats and cheeses.*

# Roasted Allium Confit

*This confit is so sweet, earthy, and redolent of alliums that we eat it straight from the jar and use it in an Arabian Nights' number of ways. Serve it with any meat, fish, poultry, or vegetable. Eat it with bread and cheese. Mix it into pasta, potato, chicken, or tuna salad. Give a jar to your best friend. Finely chop it and use it in a vinaigrette, in scrambled eggs or an omelette, or as a garnish for soup. For a flavorful onion dip, mix 1 cup (240 ml) chopped confit with 1 cup (240 ml) sour cream, a dash or two of Tabasco sauce, and salt and freshly ground pepper to taste.*

3 pounds (1.4 kg) onions, both sweet and hot, red, yellow, or white
1 1/2 pounds (675 g) leeks
1/2 pound (225 g) shallots

1/2 cup (120 ml) extra-virgin olive oil
Generous handful thyme sprigs
Salt and freshly ground black pepper

Preheat the oven to 400°F (200°C). Drizzle a jelly roll pan or large, heavy-duty baking sheet with sides with 1 tablespoon (15 ml) oil.

Trim the leeks to the pale tender green, halve lengthwise, rinse well, and cut crosswise into 3/8-inch (8-mm) slices. Peel the shallots; leave them whole if they are small or halve them lengthwise if they are large. Peel the onions and halve them lengthwise. Slice the halves lengthwise into slices about 1/4 inch (5 mm) thick.

Spread half of the onions in the pan. Scatter the thyme sprigs over them. Sprinkle the leeks and shallots over the onions. Generously salt and pepper the alliums and drizzle one-third of the olive oil over them. Spread the remaining onions on top. Generously season with salt and pepper and drizzle the rest of the olive oil over them. The pan will be very full, but the alliums will cook down.

Place the pan in the center of the oven and roast 15 minutes. Turn the alliums with a metal spatula. Reduce the temperature to 325°F (160°C) and roast 50 to 60 minutes longer, turning the alliums a few times during cooking. They should be soft and tender, with some golden brown edges.

Let the alliums cool on the baking pan. Remove the thyme stems and pack the allium confit in sterilized jars, sealing them with sterile lids and rings. Store them in the refrigerator as long as 2 weeks.

# GRILLED ONIONS

3 pounds (1.4 kg) sweet onions
1/2 cup (120 ml) olive oil
Salt and freshly ground pepper

Prepare a medium-hot charcoal fire in your grill or preheat the broiler.

Trim the root and stem ends from the onions. Slice the onions crosswise 3/4 to 1 inch (1 to 2 cm) thick. If you like, skewer the slices through the center for charcoal grilling. This is a good idea if the onions are not very fresh and tight.

Brush the onions lightly with the oil on both sides and season with salt and pepper. Grill the onions over the charcoal, turning them frequently, about 10 minutes, or until they are well-colored and crisp-tender.

If you are broiling the onions, adjust the rack so that the onions will be about 5 inches (13 cm) from the flame. Oil and season the onions as above and arrange them on a lightly oiled broiler pan in a single layer.

Broil 5 minutes on each side, or until the onions are deep golden brown on both sides and crisp-tender. If the onions begin to blacken, move them farther from the flame.

Remove the outer skins with tongs and place the onions on a platter. If you are serving pearl onions, let diners remove the skins. Serve hot, warm, or at room temperature.

*It's fun to grill several kinds of onions—Red Torpedoes, Texas Sweets, Mauis, Walla Wallas, Vidalias—for color and flavor differences. Pearl onions take about half as long to cook as larger sorts; you will need about 1 1/2 pounds (675 g) of them. Skewer them whole with the skins on, then watch them carefully when they are on the grill. They don't need brushing with olive oil, as the skins are removed before eating. The recipe yield is rather elastic. For ordinary mortals, we allow one medium, or half a large onion per person. For onion lovers, among whom is Susan's eight-year-old daughter Lucie, we grill a large onion per person. Frequently, we baste onion slices with a basil or tarragon vinaigrette.*

# OVEN-ROASTED SHALLOTS

Makes 6 servings or 1 generous cup (240 ml) minced shallots

*Oven-roasted shallots add wonderful flavor to soups, stews, sauces, and vinaigrettes, and they are delicious served as an accompaniment to rustic meals. They taste good with practically everything simple: plain vegetables, roasts, grills. They are so easy to prepare that giving them a recipe title is almost superfluous. (For the method of making crispy shallots, see page 18.) They keep in the refrigerator for a day or two if they are covered tightly.*

*12 medium to large red or yellow shallots, 12 ounces to 1 pound (340 to 450 g)*

Preheat the oven to 350°F (180°C). Place the shallots on a lightly oiled baking sheet. Roast them for 25 to 30 minutes, until soft, turning them halfway through the baking time.

When the shallots are cool enough to handle, cut off the root ends. You can serve the whole shallots as a garnish to an informal dinner plate. To chop or mince the shallots, first squeeze them from their skins; usually you will lose the outer layer of flesh along with the skin. Chop or mince the shallots and use them as desired.

# DESSERTS

*Allium Upside-Down Cake*

# ALLIUM UPSIDE-DOWN CAKE

Makes a 10-inch (25-cm) cake

Serves 8 to 12

*Even unadventuresome eaters ask for seconds of this cake. The buttermilk adds a bit of tangy contrast to the onions while the coriander seed gives a hint of soft spiciness and citrus. We usually don't have any of this to store, but when we do, we keep it wrapped in foil at cool room temperature.*

4 tablespoons (60 ml) unsalted butter

1/2 cup (120 ml) packed dark brown sugar

2 medium Vidalia, Walla Walla, Texas Sweet, or Maui onions

2 1/4 cups (540 ml) unbleached flour

1/2 teaspoon (2 ml) salt

2 1/2 teaspoons (12 ml) baking powder

3/4 teaspoon (4 ml) baking soda

1 teaspoon (5 ml) fresh ground coriander seed

4 tablespoons (60 ml) unsalted butter, softened

1 cup (240 ml) sugar

3 extra-large eggs

1 1/2 cups (360 ml) buttermilk

Melt 4 tablespoons (60 ml) butter in a 10-inch (25-cm) iron skillet over medium-low heat. Add the brown sugar and stir to dissolve; the mixture should look like thick chocolate syrup. As soon as the mixture starts to bubble, remove the pan from heat.

Peel the onions, cut them in half lengthwise, then crosswise into slices 1/4 inch (5 cm) thick. Arrange the onion slices close together in a decorative pattern in the skillet on top of the sugar mixture. Reserve any leftover slices for another use.

Preheat the oven to 375°F (190°C). Combine the flour, salt, baking powder, baking soda, and coriander together in a bowl.

In a mixing bowl, beat the softened butter. Add the sugar and beat until well combined, stopping to scrape the sides of the bowl. Add the eggs, one at a time, beating well after each addition. Add the buttermilk and beat until blended.

Add the dry ingredients to the buttermilk mixture and beat, scraping the sides of the bowl, until the batter is smooth. Pour the batter over the onions in the skillet.

Bake in the center of the oven 15 minutes. Lower the heat to 350°F (180°C) and bake 25 minutes longer, or until top is golden brown, the edges have pulled slightly from the sides of the pan, and a tester comes out clean.

Remove the cake from the oven and carefully run a metal spatula around the edges. Place a cake plate over the skillet and carefully turn the cake out onto the plate. It should come out easily; rearrange any onion slices that became dislodged. Scrape any excess topping in the skillet onto the cake. Let the cake cool for at least 20 minutes before serving. We like it slightly warm or at room temperature.

# Sweet Onion and Poppy-Seed Loaf

*This delectable loaf is good with tea, at breakfast, or as a snack. When we were developing this recipe, we could taste it in our minds' palates, but even we were surprised at how good it is. But don't take our word for it—break through conceptual dessert barriers and try it. Any mild, sweet onion can be used—Maui, Texas Sweet, Vidalia, or Walla Walla. The loaves freeze well, and the small ones are nice little house presents when you go visiting.*

1 medium-sized sweet onion, about 8 ounces (225 g)
8 tablespoons (120 ml) unsalted butter, softened
4 cups (950 ml) unbleached white flour
2 teaspoons (10 ml) baking powder
1/2 teaspoon (2 ml) baking soda
Generous 1/2 (2 ml) teaspoon salt
1/2 cup (120 ml) canola, peanut or vegetable oil
1 cup (240 ml) sugar
4 extra-large eggs, at room temperature
1 1/2 teaspoons (8 ml) pure vanilla extract
1 cup (240 ml) milk
1/3 cup (80 ml) poppy seeds

Peel and quarter the onion lengthwise; cut each quarter crosswise into thin slices. Melt 1 tablespoon (15 ml) of the butter in a small sauté pan over medium heat. Add the onion and stir 2 minutes. Reduce the heat to medium low, cover the pan and sauté two to three minutes longer. Do not allow the onions to brown. Stir the onions, cover the pan, and remove from the heat.

Preheat the oven to 350°F (180°C) and lightly butter and flour two loaf pans 9 by 5 by 3 inches (23 by 13 by 8 cm) or four loaf pans 5½ by 3 by 2 inches (14 by 8 by 5 cm). Place the flour, baking powder, baking soda, and salt in a bowl and stir lightly to blend. Set aside.

In the bowl of an electric mixer, place the remaining butter and oil and beat well. Add the sugar and beat for 2 minutes longer. Add the eggs, one at a time, beating well after each addition.

Add the vanilla to the milk. On low speed, add the flour mixture in three parts to the butter mixture, alternating with the milk, and beat until the batter is just smooth. Sprinkle the poppy seeds over the batter, add the onions, and fold them in with a rubber spatula until they are just blended.

Divide the batter among the loaf pans and spread it evenly. Bake the loaves in the center of the oven; small loaves take 25 to 35 minutes and larger ones, 45 to 50 minutes. The loaves are done when a tester comes out clean, the tops are golden brown, and the edges have pulled slightly from the sides of the pan.

Remove the loaves from their pans and cool them on a baking rack. Serve slightly warm or at room temperature. You may store the loaves for a day or two at cool room temperature. To store as long as 3 months, wrap in plastic wrap, then in foil and freeze. Defrost the loaves at room temperature.

# BIBLIOGRAPHY

## Books

Batcheller, Barbara. *Lilies of the Kitchen*. New York: St. Martin's Press, 1986.

Creasy, Rosalind. *Cooking From the Garden*. San Francisco: Sierra Club Books, 1988.

Griffith, Linda and Fred. *Onions, Onions, Onions*. Shelbuurne, VT: Chapters Publishing Ltd., 1994.

Grigson, Jane. *Jane Grigson's Vegetable Book*. New York: Penguin Books, 1978.

Phillips, Roger, and Rix, Martyn. *The Random House Book of Vegetables*. New York: Random House, 1993.

Root, Waverly. *Food*. New York: Simon and Schuster, 1980.

Stobart, Tom. *Herbs, Spices, and Flavorings*. Woodstock, NY: Overlook Press, 1982.

Taylor, Norman. *Taylor's Guide to Vegetables and Herbs*. Revised and edited by Grodon P. DeWolf, Jr. Boston: Houghton Mifflin, 1987.

Toussaint-Samat, Maguelonne. *A History of Food*. Translated by Anthea Bell. Cambridge, Massachusetts: Blackwell Publishers, 1992.

## Periodicals

Belsinger, Susan and Carolyn Dille. "The Onion Family." *The Herb Companion*, February-March, 1995, pp. 36–43.

Block, Eric. "Slicing New Sulfur Compounds." *Science News*, June 16, 1990, p. 380.

———. "The Chemistry of Garlic and Onions." *Scientific American*, March 1985, pp. 114–19.

Cook, Jack. "Onion Savvy." *Organic Gardening*, July-August 1990, pp. 28–33.

National Garden Bureau. "1995 as the Year of the Onion." *National Garden Bureau*, 1995.

Peterson, Cass. "For Onion Gardeners, Sweet Success Must Be a Long Day's Pursuit." *New York Times*, February 12, 1995, p. 47.

Pierce, B.H. "The Vidalia Onion." *Gourmet*, November, 1991, pp. 142–143.

Poncavage, Joanna. "Optimum Onions!" *Organic Gardening*, November 1993, pp. 42–47.

Radcliffe Culinary Friends of the Schlesinger Library. "Onions." *Radcliffe Culinary Times*, Summer 1994, p. 6.

Ritchie, James D. "Do You Know Your Onions?" *Flower and Garden*, May 1994, pp. 58–61.

# SOURCES

Bountiful Gardens, 1801 Shafer Ranch Road, Willits, CA 95490-9626

Burpee and Company, W. Atlee, Warminster, PA 1897 (800) 888-1447

Cook's Garden, P.O. Box 535 Londonderry, VT 05148, (802) 824-3400

Dutch Gardens, P.O. Box 200, Adelphia, NJ 07710-0200, (908) 780-27113

Hudson, J.L., Seedsman, P.O. Box 1058, Redwood City, CA 94064

Johnny's Selected Seeds, Foss Hill Road, Albion, ME 04910-9731, (207) 437-4301

Kalmia Farm, P.O. Box 3881, Charlottesville, VA 22903-0881

Nichols Garden Nursery, 1190 North Pacific Highway, Albany, OR 97321-4598

Park Seed Company, Cokesbury Road, Greenwood, SC 29647-0001, (803) 223-7333

Pinetree Garden Seeds, Box 300, New Gloucester, ME 04260, (207) 926-3400

Ronniger's, Star Route, Moyie Springs, ID 83845

Seeds of Change, P.O. Box 15700, Santa Fe, NM 87506-5700, (505) 438-8080

Shepherd's Garden Seeds, 30 Irene Street, Torrington, CT 06790, (203) 482-3638

Territorial Seed Company, P.O. Box 157, Cottage Grove, OR 97424-0061, (503) 942-9547

# INDEX

bacteria 34
Blanco Duro 33, 34
Bleu de Solaise 33
boiling onions 14
bolting 28
Borettana Cipolline 33
breath 14
bulb onions 15
bunching onions 10
Cambodian cuisine 18
champ 17
Chinese 16
ciboules 10
cipolline 15
Crystal Wax 33
curing 34–36
cutting onions 21
day-length requirements 26–28
dicing onions 22
digestibility 14
Dutch Yellow 33
Early Aviv Pearl 33
Ebenezer 34
Egyptian 32
Emerald Isle 33
Fall Giant 33
fertilizing 26
fiber in onions 12
French Grey 15, 33
French Red 33
fresh onions 15
Frog's Leg 15, 33
fungi 34
Gerard 9
Giant Winter 33
Golden Gemet 33
Granex 33
grated onion 24
grilling onions 21
growing conditions 26–29

growing from plants 29
growing from seed 29–30
growing from sets 29
growing temperatures 28–29
harvesting 33–36
health benefits 11–13
heirloom seed 30
Hemingway, Ernest 17
hybrids 30, 33
Indonesian cuisine 18
Japanese 16
King Richard 33
leeks 15
leeks, cooking with 20–21
leeks, trimming and cleaning 22
mashed potatoes 17
Maui 15, 33
mignonette 18
National Garden Bureau 28
onion juice 24
organically grown seed 30
overwintering 28–29
oyster sauce 18
pearl onions 8, 15
pests 26
Pliny the Elder 10–11
potassium 12
potato onions 15, 33
ramps 32
raw onion sandwich 17
Red Beard 33
Red Creole 34
Red Sun 33
red wine and onions 19
scallions 10, 16
scallions, cooking with 17–18
seed 29–30
sets 29
shallots 15
shallot, crispy fried 18

shallots in sauces 18
Singapore cuisine 18
soil properties 25
soubise 19
sowing indoors 30
sowing outdoors 30
Stockton Red 33
storage 22–24, 33–34
storage humidity 22
storage temperatures 22
storage, long-term 22, 33–34
Stuttgarter 33, 34
sulfides 13
sulfur compounds 12
sulfur, hotness and 31–32
sweet onions 15
Sweet Sandwich 33
Swift, Jonathan 14
tearing factor 13, 21
Texas Sweet 1015 15, 33
Thai cuisine 18
thrips 26
Titan 33
Tokyo Long White 33
tops, pushing down 34
Torpedo Bottle 33
transplanting 30–31
Tree onion 32
Tu Fu 10
Vidalia 15, 19
vitamin A 12
vitamin C 12
Walking 32
Walla Walla 15, 33
weeding 26
Welsh onions 10, 16
White Lisbon 33
winter onions 10
Yellow Torque 34
Yula 34

# Recipe Index

## BREADS, APPETIZERS, AND FIRST COURSES

Buttermilk Biscuits with Scallions
and Parmesan Cheese 42
Chèvre with Shallots 44
Focaccia with Onions and
Rosemary 40
Green Onion Focaccia 38
Maui Onion Tart 43
Onion Rings, Chesapeake Style 45

## SOUPS AND PASTA

Italian-Style Bread and Onion
Soup 51
Leek and Chick-Pea Soup 47
Onion and Noodle Kugel with
Herbs 54
Onion Family Soup 50
Roasted Onion and Corn Chowder
with Poblano Chile Cream 48
Sauté of Leeks, Endive, and
Radicchio with Linguine 52

## MAIN COURSES

Mussels with Shallots, Onions, and
Thyme 64
Onion Tomato Pie 57
Polenta with Onions, Spinach, and
Blue Cheese 61
Rice with Leeks and Mushrooms
63
Roast Chicken Stuffed with Leeks,
Shallots, and Tarragon 63
Southwestern Grits, Onion, and
Chile Casserole 59
Steak Smothered with Balsamic
Onions 67

## VEGETABLES AND SALADS

Baked Onions, Southern Italian
Style 70
Leek and Celery Root Gratin with
Horseradish 75
Onion and Cucumber Salad 76
Orange and Onion Salad 78
Potato Salad with Scallions and
Red Peppers 77
Roasted Onions, Artichokes, and
Potatoes 72
Sauerkraut with Onions 74
Wine and Vinegar Glazed
Onions 73

## SAUCES, ACCOMPANIMENTS, AND CONDIMENTS

Green Onion Vinaigrette 83
Grilled Onions 87
Onion Mushroom Gravy 80
Oven-Roasted Shallots 88
Pickled Onions 85
Roasted Allium Confit 86
Shallot Vinaigrette 82
Tunisian-Style Relish 84

## DESSERTS

Allium Upside-Down Cake 90
Sweet Onion and Poppy-Seed
Loaf 92